Quebec and Related Silver at The Detroit Institute of Arts

Quebec and Related Silver
at The Detroit Institute of Arts

by Ross Allan C. Fox
The Detroit Institute of Arts

Published for Founders Society Detroit Institute of Arts by Wayne State University Press   Detroit, 1978

Library of Congress Cataloging in Publication Data
Detroit. Institute of Arts.
  Quebec and related silver at the Detroit Institute of Arts.

  Includes bibliographical references and index.
  1. Silverwork—Québec (Province)—Catalogs.
  2. Church plate—Québec (Province)—Catalogs.
  3. Silversmiths—Québec (Province)—Biography.
  4. Detroit. Institute of Arts. I. Fox, Ross Allan C., 1945–   II. Founders Society. III. Title.
  NK7113.A3Q33   739.2'3'7714074017434   77-4850
  ISBN 0-8143-1575-5

All photographs by E. Irving Blomstrann except the following: Henry Birks Collection (figs. 27, 44); Detroit Institute of Arts (figs. 11, 12, 54); Inventaire des Biens Culturels, Quebec City (figs. 6, 41); National Gallery of Canada, Ottawa (figs. 9, 21, 24, 25, 42, 56, 58); author (figs. 2, 4, 5, 17, 19, 22, 23, 26, 32, 33, 39, 40).

Contents

Publication of this catalogue
has been made possible
through the generosity of the
Elizabeth, Allan, and
Warren Shelden Fund

Foreword

In 1946 The Detroit Institute of Arts organized the exhibition *The Arts of French Canada*. The first major exhibition dedicated to this subject, it traveled to other American and Canadian cities and introduced the public to a little-known but rich early North American artistic tradition. Its impact on scholars and on the study of Canadian art has been immeasurable. Since that significant event in the historiography of French Canadian art, interest has greatly intensified, and quality pieces are now found only in museums, churches, and a few large private collections. The Detroit Institute of Arts has a very fine collection, the largest of its kind outside of Canada. An important aspect of this collection is its silver.

The initial creation and subsequent expansion of this collection of French Canadian silver was made possible through the generosity of numerous patrons, particularly Mrs. Allan Shelden and the late Robert H. Tannahill. Mrs. Allan Shelden III and her late husband, Allan Shelden III, were also very supportive of this interest, adding significant pieces to the collection. It is also the Shelden Family Fund which has made possible the publication of this catalogue. Also deserving special mention are Mr. and Mrs. William J. Marcoux and Verner W. Crane, who have loaned pieces in this catalogue (Nos. 18 and 23).

In this study of the French Canadian silver at Detroit, Ross Fox has provided not only a meticulous examination of each object but also a much-needed general introduction to the subject, which will be appreciated by both layman and scholar. The catalogue will be welcomed as a step forward in the study of Canadian silver and of Canadian art in general.

Frederick J. Cummings, *Director*
The Detroit Institute of Arts

Preface

In the early seventeenth century French culture was planted in America on the banks of the Saint Lawrence River. From the outset, the harsh physical environment and the disinterest of the mother country made survival precarious. Eventually it was surrounded and almost submerged by a multitude of culturally unsympathetic English-speaking people, yet after almost four hundred years, Quebec remains the largest concentration of people of French culture and race outside of France. Time and isolation have given this community a distinct and immutable identity: the French culture of Quebec and Canada is also uniquely North American. Its character is reflected in its early arts, and the art of the silversmith is important among them.

Quebec silver is not well known to Americans, and so this catalogue is intended both as a comprehensive study of the Detroit collection and as a general introduction. Although there are, unfortunately, no pieces in the collection by those two highly significant eighteenth-century silversmiths François Ranvoyzé and Ignace-François Delezenne, most of the important makers are represented here. The first four objects in the catalogue are French pieces by anonymous makers which were imported into New France in the late seventeenth and early eighteenth centuries. The next two pieces are also by anonymous makers, the first made in either France or Quebec, the second probably made in Quebec. The remaining silver is by Quebec silversmiths.

The discussion of the role of silver in society, which precedes the catalogue entries, attempts, for the first time, to delineate the styles and stylistic sequences of Quebec silver. This classification is intended merely as a framework for general stylistic analysis, and refinements will undoubtedly be made in the future as even more pieces are studied. It should be noted that French styles are cited only when they relate to French silver made for the Canadian market or help to explain styles in Quebec.

Much is yet to be learned about the lives of most of the silversmiths represented in the Detroit collection. The brief biography which introduces the work of each silversmith is, in many cases, necessarily incomplete and based on secondary sources; however, in some cases hitherto unpublished archival materials have been drawn upon to round out our knowledge of the artist.

Each piece represented has been dated as accurately as possible and has been placed within the context of the maker's production and the Quebec silver craft. Dating remains problematic: few pieces in other collections have been fully researched, and suitably dated comparative material is thus scarce. Moreover, only in rare instances, chiefly in the case of church silver, can original documents pertaining to a specific piece be located. Pieces are in good condition unless otherwise noted.

In describing the construction of each piece and the techniques employed in fashioning it, elemental composition (the respective percentages of silver, gold, and base metals) is given when it helps resolve the authenticity of a part or parts. The quantitative elemental analysis of most pieces was undertaken at the Conservation Laboratory of the Henry Francis du Pont Winterthur Museum. The results of that study are summarized in an appendix. The Winterthur analysis was also instrumental in the resolution of some uncertain attributions. That analysis represents a major contribution to the study of Quebec silver and has not previously been included in a catalogue devoted to silver.

Recently there has been a deluge of forged Canadian silver. Some fakes have been identified in the Detroit collection; others may have been overlooked. Marks with no precedent should be regarded with a skeptical eye: for example, the marks on Nos. 27, 34, and 38 here require further study. Comprehensive studies of all the variations of the leading silversmiths' marks have not yet been made, and this is one more task facing future researchers of Quebec silver.

Acknowledgments

Publication of this catalogue was made possible through the interest and generous patronage of Mrs. Allan Shelden. Mrs. Shelden has been the principal agent in the tremendous expansion of the collection of French Canadian art at the Detroit Institute of Arts during the last two decades. My thanks go to Frederick J. Cummings, who first conceived of this project and then supported it with patience and enthusiasm.

The comprehensive elemental analysis was done at the Henry Francis du Pont Winterthur Museum by Victor F. Hanson, Coordinator and Head of Scientific Research, and his two assistants, Janice H. Carlson and Karen Papouchado. Studies of this sort by Mr. Hanson and his associates have been key factors in increasing the sophistication of our knowledge of the decorative arts. He was also kind enough to read this manuscript and to offer his criticism of my analysis.

Francis W. Robinson, Curator Emeritus of Medieval Art, Detroit Institute of Arts, whose manifold areas of expertise include French Canadian art, introduced me to this artistic tradition, supplied many materials, of which the most important are related to pieces produced for Detroit and to silversmiths active there, and read the final typescript. Jean Trudel, conservateur de l'art canadien ancien, National Gallery of Canada, Ottawa, reviewed the typescript, and his advice on many doubtful points is greatly appreciated.

The research for this catalogue, particularly the verification of provenance and the use of comparative material, would not have been possible without the assistance of the staffs of the Musée du Québec and the Inventaire des Biens Culturels, both in Quebec City. Particular thanks go to André Juneau, directeur, and Claude Thibault, conservateur-adjoint de l'art ancien du Québec, of the Musée du Québec, and to Michel Cauchon, directeur, Inventaire des Biens Culturels.

The Conservation Laboratory at The Detroit Institute of Arts, James Greaves, Chief Conservator, and Meryl

Johnson, Associate Conservator, Technical Research, were of great help. Ms. Johnson and I spent many hours examining pieces under a microscope in an effort to determine the precise silversmithing techniques employed. She also helped in the interpretation of the elemental analysis and reviewed the typescript.

I am indebted to John E. Langdon, of Toronto, for his critique of the typescript and his suggestions regarding the biographies; to William H. Peck, Curator of Ancient Art, Detroit Institute of Arts, for his encouragement and moral support of a project entirely unrelated to my duties as his assistant; to Susan Rossen and Rollyn Krichbaum, of the Publications Department, Detroit Institute of Arts; to E. Irving Blomstrann, New Britain, Conn., who photographed most of the objects; and to Ruth Anne Labonté Fox, my wife, who assisted in everything from searching through archival sources to proofreading.

Special thanks are also extended to Wayne Andrews, Roland-J. Auger, Henry G. Birks, Marcella Christopher, Charles H. Elam, Donald Fenemore, Phillip Fike, Raymond Gingras, Thelma M. Graham, Joseph Gutmann, S. N. Hlopoff, Helena Ignatieff, Gilberte Letourneau, Andrew Oliver, Jr., and John L. Russell.

Silver and Society

In the European society of the seventeenth and eighteenth centuries, silver was owned almost exclusively by the wealthier classes. In American society, whether English or French, as the general standard of living was higher, it was more common but was still owned and used in any quantity only by a very small percentage of the population. In French colonial society, where Roman Catholicism was the official and only religion, the sacred vessels of churches extended its use and importance.

Domestic plate served a special function in a society in which survival in a harsh and isolated environment was of uppermost concern. Moneyed colonists felt little need for the sculpture, paintings, and *objets de luxe* of the salons of Paris. Silver plate was a more practical investment: it was an outward symbol of social prestige and material success, and it was utilitarian, portable, and readily convertible into currency, important considerations in a colonial society. Although much less domestic silver survives in Quebec than in New England, this fact does not accurately reflect its importance in New France, for the population of the French colony was only a small fraction of that of the English.[1]

Even some of the earliest settlers possessed modest amounts of silver. For example, when Antoine de la Fresnaye, Sieur de Brucy, a seigneur, officer, and merchant of Montreal, died in 1684, he left silver plate weighing 109 ounces and valued at 470 livres.[2] By the early eighteenth century many prominent colonial personalities had quite extensive holdings. The 1726 inventory of Philippe de Rigaud, Marquis de Vaudreuil, governor of New France, lists over 1,260 ounces of plate.[3] The gentlemen-bourgeois of New France, a landowning and commercial gentry some of whom were nobles, generally lived in comfortable circumstances, especially in the latter decades of the French regime. Most of their luxuries were imported, including much of their silver, some of which came from fine Parisian workshops. The more modest requirements of the small merchants and artisans furnished the bulk of the domestic trade of the colonial silversmiths—items such as spoons, forks, tumblers, ladles, écuelles, and occasionally plates or candlesticks.

The church supplied silversmiths with most of their larger and more important commissions. Its canonical requirements specified that chalices (communion cups) must be fashioned from one of the most precious metals, either gold or silver. As silver was the cheapest and most readily available, it was most popular. The church also encouraged the use of silver in all vessels associated with the Mass. Although most early churches possessed only a silver chalice, as they prospered their communion plate grew to include a great variety of silver vessels. In fact, in the eighteenth and nineteenth centuries the rural parish churches of Quebec were generally much better endowed with sacred vessels and other ecclesiastical furnishings than were their counterparts in France. During the French regime, most silver church vessels were apparently imported from France.[4]

With the British conquest of New France in 1759, the social character of the colony was dramatically transformed. The French gentlemen-bourgeois were supplanted in the colonial administration by royal appointees from England and in commerce by English merchants, many of whom came from the American colonies. Excluded from many of their traditional functions, the French gentlemen-bourgeois turned to such professions as medicine, law, and surveying. The new dominance of the English was soon reinforced by refugees from the American colonies; by 1792, there were 10,000 English and 145,000 French in Quebec. During the next century, the essential social fabric was to remain fixed, with an English minority dominant in government and commerce and a subordinate French majority with its own native leadership of bourgeois professionals.

The early British regime was relatively stable, and its economic prosperity derived from an expanded fur trade in the northwest, especially from 1790 to 1808. After the War of 1812, social and economic conditions deteriorated, partially because the fur trade had moved farther west. During the early period of British rule, silver retained its importance in the colonial culture. Again, it was the bourgeoisie, now both French and English, who were the chief domestic customers of the Quebec silversmiths. Like their French predecessors, the English gentry preferred to import their silver and other luxuries from the mother country. The bourgeoisie, imitating the fashions of the upper class, commissioned plate in the current English styles from colonial silversmiths.

From 1759 to the second quarter of the nineteenth century, the ecclesiastical trade was almost entirely in the hands of local silversmiths. All church art in Quebec, including silver, continued to conform to French design, as was required by the clerical patrons. In the late eighteenth century the Catholic clergy remained strongly pro-French and pro-monarchist, and these attitudes were strengthened by the arrival of a large number of French clerics in 1802, refugees from the French Revolution who had been detained in England. After the restoration of the French monarchy in 1816, these clerics initiated renewed contacts between the clergy of France and Quebec; the interaction between the two was closest in the 1850s and 1860s. The result was renewed importation of religious art from France, and Quebec silversmiths experienced an increasing loss in their ecclesiastical trade from the 1830s on.

The Silversmiths

The extremely small population of New France in the seventeenth century could not support an active local silver trade, and all early silver was imported from Paris. This practice, which continued into the eighteenth century, retarded the development of a viable colonial craft, but an even more important factor was the inadequate supply of raw material. There were no silver deposits in the colony, and only coin and worn-out plate, both in short supply, were available to the silversmith.

In the late seventeenth century a few gunsmith-silversmiths were active, but for the most part they confined themselves to the repair of French pieces. The first professional silversmith to settle in New France was Michel Levasseur, who worked in Quebec City from about 1700 to 1712, when he returned to France. He trained two apprentices, Pierre Gauvreau and Jacques Pagé dit Quercy, and a colonial craft was established. During the second and third decades of the century other silversmiths arrived from France, including François Chambellan and Roland Paradis from Paris, Paul Lambert dit Saint-Paul from Arras, and Jean-Baptiste Deschevery dit Maisonbasse from Bayonne. However, many craftsmen, among them Michel Cotton and Jean-François Landron, were born and trained in Canada.

Early commissions were relatively meager: most silver was still imported, and all silversmiths except Lambert were forced to engage in some other activity to earn a living. Many were gunsmiths, merchants, or jewelers. The economic prosperity of the 1740s benefited these silversmiths, but their customers were still largely the bourgeoisie and rural parish churches. About 1755, however, silver ornaments began to be made for the Indian trade in vast quantities: on 31 May 1758, the silversmith Ignace-François Delezenne engaged another silversmith, Jean Robaille, to make 8,000 ounces of silver trinkets.[5] Indian trade silver assumed even greater importance at the end of the century

and remained one of the mainstays of Quebec silversmiths until the second quarter of the nineteenth century.

After the British conquest, when Quebec silversmiths found themselves with a near-monopoly of the ecclesiastical trade and a greatly expanded domestic trade, Canadian-trained silversmiths, including Joseph Maillou, Jacques Varin, and François Ranvoyzé, were at hand, but new immigrants also followed in the wake of the British armies. Among the new arrivals were Robert Cruickshank from Great Britain, Joseph Schindler from Switzerland, James Hanna from Ireland, David Bohle from Germany, and, after the American Revolution, Isaac Clements from New York. A few silversmiths dominated the markets of the two most important cities, Quebec and Montreal. Ranvoyzé monopolized the trade of the Quebec City region until 1787, when he was gradually replaced by Laurent Amiot. Montreal had a large number of silversmiths, but Robert Cruickshank and Pierre Huguet dit Latour, both operating large workshops, were the undisputed masters.

Indian trade silver was of special importance to Montreal silversmiths in this period. Many of these silversmiths began to follow the fur trade west, and many settled in Detroit, which was under British rule until 1796. In the early eighteenth century, a few Quebec gunsmith-silversmiths had come to this important stopping point on the route west, including Pierre Belleperche and Pierre Barthe. Now there was a minor influx which brought Amable Maillou, Dominique Rousseau, Jean-Baptiste Piquette, and Augustin Lagrave. Many eventually moved even farther west to the territories of Indiana and Missouri.

After the War of 1812, the loss of the market for Indian trade silver and generally depressed economic conditions marked the beginning of the decline of Quebec silversmiths. By the second quarter of the nineteenth century, Montreal had only two important silversmiths, Salomon Marion and Paul Morand. In Quebec City, there was Amiot, who after 1839 was succeeded by François Sasseville, his former apprentice. With Sasseville's death in 1864, the craft essentially came to an end, although a few minor artisans were active in Quebec until the end of the century. It succumbed to its competition. In the 1830s, renewed importation of silver, domestic from England and ecclesiastical from France, increasingly encroached on the Quebec market, but it was the inexpensive wares of silver manufacturers, who were now also producing plated silver, which sealed the fate of the traditional craftsmen. These new silver manufacturers, makers to the trade, proliferated in the third quarter of the nineteenth century; the most important of them was Robert Hendery and his firm of Hendery and Leslie, which was bought out by Henry Birks & Sons in 1899.

Stylistic Origins

The stylistic sources for Quebec silver are found in France and England. French styles were followed before 1763; thereafter a dual character evolves, with domestic silver increasingly imitating English taste, while ecclesiastical silver remains largely French. At no time was there a uniquely Canadian or Quebec style, although individual silversmiths sometimes produced personal interpretations of French designs.

Early Quebec silversmiths had access to French models from the plate—largely provincial—that colonists brought with them, and from imports, which were generally Parisian. Other designs were introduced more directly by immigrant silversmiths. While it is French, the character of early colonial silver is also manifestly provincial. Changes in French fashion originated in the court circles of Versailles and Paris, and several decades usually ensued before a new style was fully assimilated by the French provinces. Coexisting with the prevailing fashion, whether in Paris or in the provinces, was a retardataire undercurrent which

adhered to plain substantial forms and outmoded designs and was typical of the work of lesser silversmiths for a clientele of modest means. In New France, however, this retardataire aspect was not an undercurrent but the dominant element; it is only partially explained by the extreme isolation of the colony and the modest commissions of the colonists. The standard of colonial craftsmanship, or the lack thereof, was another contributing factor. There was no officially imposed standard, whereas, in each city of France, every aspect of silver production was supervised by a local guild, entrance to which was restricted by a rigid quota system. Some of the silversmiths who emigrated to New France undoubtedly did so because they had failed to gain admittance to the guilds in their native cities. Emigration was one of the few alternatives remaining if they wished to practice their craft. The type and duration of training of silversmiths in the colony varied greatly, and sometimes a silversmith was even self-taught. Thus, while their workmanship was often very competent, the absence of enforced craft standards sometimes resulted in work which was inferior in quality to that of most French provinces.

The earliest surviving French silver in Quebec, largely ecclesiastical, dates from the second and third quarters of the seventeenth century. The style is that of Louis XIII, a style which flourished in Paris during the period (see No. 1). A late manifestation of Renaissance design, this style is distinguished by a formal all-over decoration of embossed scrollwork, foliate ornament such as rinceaux, acanthus, and palmettes, garlands, masks, and putti. As the colonial craft did not develop until the early eighteenth century, the overall effect of this style was minimal and was very much subordinate to the succeeding Louis XIV style, which prevailed in Quebec until the last decades of the 18th century.

The opulent ''baroque'' Louis XIV style was largely restricted to Versailles; however, a restrained derivative was popular in France. Developed by the 1660s, it was characterized by a reduction in formal ornament, using instead bands of foliate ornament, beading, fluting, gadrooning, and cutcard work alternated with plain bands. After the royal proscriptions of 1689 against the use of silver in monumental objects, especially furniture, the decoration of smaller objects assumed a new importance. The earlier divisioning into registers and panels, often outlined by moldings, was retained, but plain surfaces were usually replaced by delicately engraved bands of interlace, foliate scrollwork, or diaperwork. Applied strapwork or guilloche bands were also employed.

This style dominated Parisian domestic silver until about 1730 and, due to the inherent conservatism of church art, continued in ecclesiastical use until about 1750. Late Louis XIV ecclesiastical plate developed a severity of profile, with bands of extensive gadrooning, beading, reeding, and dentiling alternating with plain, taut, highly burnished surfaces (No. 16). Colonial silversmiths derived their inspiration for ecclesiastical plate from both the Louis XIII and Louis XIV styles, but chiefly the latter. Sometimes elements of both styles were combined rather indiscriminately. Domestic silver usually followed plainer Louis XIV designs (No. 6), even at the peak of the Rococo style in France during the 1740s and 1750s. The fluid organic forms of Rococo silver were usually embellished with naturalistic foliate and floral ornament, shellwork, crustacea, and spiral fluting. Although some fine specimens of the style entered the colony (Nos. 3 and 4), it was never adopted by colonial silversmiths except for an occasional minor flourish, as in the fluted rayed handles of écuelles or the scrolled feet of salts.

Louis XIV designs persisted in Quebec after 1759, in domestic silver as late as 1790, and in ecclesiastical work until about 1810 at Quebec City and even later at Montreal. Thus, in the immediate post-conquest period, the earlier retardataire aspect of French colonial silver was not only maintained but intensified because of the forced severance of political ties with France and an almost complete halt to French silver imports. As more current French designs were no longer available to colonial silversmiths, old French pieces already in the colony remained the principal design source. These old pieces were not necessarily copied without imagination; for example, François Ranvoyzé instilled in Louis XIII formal patterns a free-flowing vivacity which was uniquely his own. Clerical patrons were also an important factor in the retention of Louis XIV designs. When adding to his communion plate, a priest would frequently specify that a silversmith copy an early French vessel already in his church.

The British conquest resulted in a stylistic division between ecclesiastical and domestic designs, the former French, the latter English. Although not immediately apparent, this French-English duality distinguishes Quebec silver after about 1790–1800. English designs were transmitted either directly, through English and American silversmiths, or through English imports. From about 1790 until after 1820, domestic silver was essentially in the English Neoclassic style (see No. 18). Under the influence of the classical aesthetic of Robert Adam and the development of machine-rolled sheets of silver, holloware was fashioned into classical forms with taut, smooth surfaces. Ornament was used sparingly and was usually bright-cut, including garlands, ribbons, and pendants.

After about 1790, two distinct regional schools of ecclesiastical silver can be discerned, one centered at Quebec City, the other at Montreal. The Quebec school turned to the Louis XVI style, the French equivalent of the English Neoclassic. The Montreal school is not so easily defined, as there were numerous stylistic cross-influences, owing largely to the more varied background and training of the silversmiths active there. However, the Louis XIV style predominates in church silver of the late eighteenth and early nineteenth centuries. The division of Quebec into two regional schools, each distinguished by style, finds a contemporary parallel with sculpture. From the 1790s on, church decoration of the Quebec City region was largely in the Neoclassic style of the Baillairgés, while Montreal followed the retardataire Rococo style of Philippe Liébert and then of Louis Quévillon.

Laurent Amiot introduced the Louis XVI style to Quebec upon his return from Paris in 1787. It soon became the preferred style for church silver at Quebec City (No. 8). Amiot also produced a few exceptional domestic pieces in the same style. Church silver relied on classical motifs such as dentils, the tongue frieze, garlands, rinceaux, and panels with embossed naturalistic floral and foliate ornament. There was also a second contrasting aspect to this style which was dependent on classically inspired forms, almost totally devoid of ornament. Louis XVI designs were being produced in Quebec as late as the 1870s by Pierre Lespérance (see No. 43, by François Sasseville).

Although Montreal silversmiths were dependent on the Louis XIV styles (see No. 25), after about 1800 they began to produce some interesting eclectic reinterpretations of Louis XVI designs. The Louis XVI style made a gradual entrance as Amiot's reputation and work became known in the upper Saint Lawrence Valley, and eventually he received a few commissions in the Montreal area. Louis XVI decoration and forms had an influence, but the finished designs of Montreal silversmiths often had little direct relationship to that style. They are best classified as being in a provincial French Neoclassic mode. As with Louis XIV designs, minor elements from the English Neoclassic style were sometimes incorporated into a design. An example of such an English design intrusion in church silver can be seen in the occasional use of bright-cut engraving (No. 26). By the 1820s Montreal silversmiths had become increasingly dependent on designs inspired by the style of Louis XVI.

In the decade which followed, the stylistic differences between the two regional schools gradually diminished, as both began to turn to the more current designs of the French Empire. The Empire style arrived with the slow renewal of French liturgical imports, which were resumed after 1816 and had become a dominant influence by the 1830s. This style was an outgrowth of Louis XVI style but also incorporated baroque elements from the Louis XIV style (No. 42). Old motifs were combined in a new way, older forms were enlarged, gilding was extensive, and there was a general overworking of ornament, which included embossed scenes from the New Testament and religious personifications. Derivatives of this style prevailed until the end of the century. The Empire style was universal; in England it was known as Regency. As an extension of the Neoclassic, it strove for archeological correctness but eventually degenerated into rather tasteless excesses in the use of classical motifs. Found on English imports to Quebec, it was adopted by Quebec silversmiths for domestic silver, but in a greatly modified form. More restrained than even the American Empire style, the Quebec forms were lighter and always retained a somewhat Neoclassic quality. The Regency style in domestic silver lasted into the 1840s.

The Rococo revival or Neo-Rococo style, a later development of the Empire and Regency styles, appeared in Quebec in the 1830s and lasted until about 1860. Rococo ornament was revived in domestic silver, but in new combinations and often in connection with Neoclassic forms (No. 34). Eventually it became a jumble of exuberant and overladen forms. The Rococo revival had only a moderate influence in Quebec and, coexisted with later manifestations of the Empire style. Rococo ornament also made slight inroads into ecclesiastical silver, as in the occasional use of scrolled ornament, which was now also engraved. After mid-century, styles became more eclectic and followed the general taste of Victorian England, the French Second Empire, and the United States.

Even in the nineteenth century Quebec society was essentially colonial, and its taste in the arts was conservative and provincial. As in most colonial societies, most luxuries were imported, and colonial artisans looked to Paris and London for innovations. In spite of the derivative styles, however, Quebec silversmiths made some fine, although rarely distinguished, domestic pieces and, in this society where religion was of paramount importance, excelled in ecclesiastical work. While we look in vain for marvels similar to those of Thomas Germain or Paul Storr, the work of Delezenne or Amiot is comparable in quality to that of Paul Revere or Joseph Richardson.

NOTES TO SILVER AND SOCIETY

1. In 1689, there were 12,000 persons in New France; in 1760, there were about 85,000. The population of the English colonies was 250,000 and 1,200,000, respectively, at these times.

2. E.-Z. Massicotte, ''Le Sieur La Fresnaye de Brucy,'' *Bulletin des Recherches Historiques* 36 (1930):644–67. Only old French weights are cited in this discussion. The old French ounce weighed 30.593 grams, as opposed to the English Troy ounce of 31.103 grams. Original currencies are also retained throughout the catalogue, as it is too difficult, if not impossible, to ascertain their approximate equivalent values in modern currency.

3. Pierre-Georges Roy, ed., ''Inventaire de Philippe de Rigaud, Marquis de Vaudreuil, Gouverneur de la Nouvelle-France,'' *Inventaire des testaments, donations et inventaires du régime français conservés aux Archives judiciaires de Québec,* III (Quebec, 1941), 189–238.

4. At present, this remains a contentious point. There is also some late eighteenth-century French silver in Quebec churches, but most was probably brought to Canada after the French Revolution by French emigré priests.

5. ANQQ, Claude Barolet minutes, 31 May 1758.

1 Ciborium, ca. 1675

MEASUREMENTS
Height 25.7 cm. (10⅛ in.); diameter of bowl 11.7 cm. (4⅝ in.); diameter of base 13 cm. (5⅛ in.); weight 640.7 gm. (20 oz. 12 dwt.)

PROVENANCE
Church of Ange-Gardien, Montmorency County, Que.; Jean Octeau, Montreal; DIA purchase 30 January 1969.

BIBLIOGRAPHY
IBC, Ange-Gardien file, photo A-8 (photographed by Gérard Morriset in 1938); Fox, "Liturgical Silver," pp. 98, 100, fig. 1.

Elizabeth, Allan, and Warren Shelden Fund (acc. no. 69.13)

DESCRIPTION
Ciborium with elaborate embossed and chased all-over decoration. The cover is raised in a low central dome and curved outer shoulder, with a chased dentiled flange and a molded vertical lip applied to the rim (fig. 1). An applied central finial of a cross with three beads and stepped pedestal is encircled by a lower applied six-petaled surround. Raying out from the petals is a star with six points, each point serving as the spine of six leaves which with six intervening leaves enwrap six gem-like bosses. The adjacent outer ornament consists of three scrolled and ribboned palmettes alternating with three husked garlands and three pendant acanthus leaves.

The plain, raised, almost hemispherical bowl has a mercury-gilt interior and an applied bead below the rim forming a bezel, or lip, to secure the cover. The bowl beneath the bead is encased in a calyx with embossed ornament similar to that of the cover, including the palmettes and garlands, an acanthus frieze below, and cable molding above. A threaded rod (actually a seamed cylinder, threaded externally), applied to the bottom of the bowl with a disc, passes through a circular perforation at the bottom of the calyx.

The baluster stem has a knop and two bead and reel collar knops. The stem proper extends as a separate unit from the upper cylinder to the lower bell form above the lower collar knop. This section is composed of over a dozen separately fashioned components, brazed together. Cylinders and discs are swaged and seamed, the knop and the lower bell form raised. The upper cylinder, threaded internally, extends into the stem and receives the threaded rod of the bowl. The upper collar knop is a plain flange with applied bead and reel band. Between the two upper knops is a two-part spool with applied beaded band at its seam and a lower stepped edge formed by two discs. The central, inverted pyriform knop has two plain bands alternating with two embossed and chased ornamental friezes. The upper plain band is actually applied to its upper shoulder, which itself has twelve small bosses partially wrapped by garlands with pendant drops and bell flowers. There is an acanthus leaf frieze on the lower knop, and below it is another applied bead and reel band and a small bell form with an applied stepped rim. The bell contains the lower threaded rod of the stem, which screws into the tangent threaded sleeve of the lower collar knop.

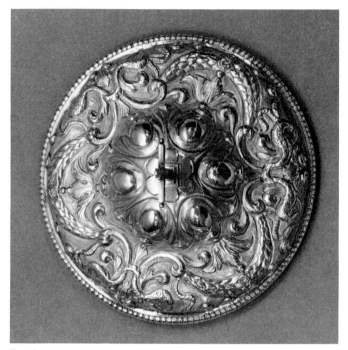

Fig. 1

This knop, repeating the bead and reel motif of the upper collar knop, is applied to a central cylinder projecting from the foot. A beaded band is applied over the join.

The domed foot is stepped and splayed; the dome repeats the motifs of cover and calyx on a reduced scale; the step has an applied dentiled flange identical to that of the cover. A flared outer openwork border consists of a frieze of acanthus leaves with tiny scrolls and spines of graduated beading; this band was stamped in a die and then cut with a piercing saw and tooled. The tips of the leaves are brazed to the drawn and seamed outer strengthening band.

Ciboria were used to carry small unleavened wafers, or hosts, during Communion and to hold them in the tabernacle on the altar at other times. Because of their sacred character, only the most precious metal was thought suitable, and the interior of the bowl must therefore be gilt, according to Roman Catholic rubrics. (The interior of the cover was frequently gilt as well.)

This ciborium was probably made in Paris, as evidenced by the design, the high silver content, and the absence of punch marks. It was once attributed to François Ranvoyzé (1739–1819) of Quebec City because of supposed stylistic affinities with a chalice bearing the mark of Ranvoyzé, also from the church of Ange-Gardien and now at the National Gallery of Canada, Ottawa (Trudel, fig. 17). However, the Detroit ciborium has a regular pattern of repeat motifs, while the chalice has a free-style or running floral decoration. Moreover, the Detroit piece is in a late version of the Louis XIII style, which ceased to be used about 1680 in Paris and about 1700 in the provinces. No Quebec silversmiths are known to have used this type of design, and no early silversmith, including Ranvoyzé, the most important Quebec silversmith of the late eighteenth century, was such a superb craftsman.

X-ray fluorescence spectroscopy (see Appendix II for an explanation of this method) reveals that the silver content of the various parts ranges from 94.66 to 97.47 percent, which lies within the range of the Paris silver standard of 95.83 percent (Carré, p. 6).

As for the marks, silver production in France was officially regulated to assure a minimum standard of craftsmanship and silver alloy content: a rigid marking system was enforced by guild wardens, who assayed the silver, and by mint contractors (*fermiers*), who collected the duty or tax on newly made silver plate. Consequently, French silver usually bore an array of marks including charge and discharge (duty) marks, maker's mark, and the guild-warden's mark. While colonial silver was exempt from this rigid marking system, it was customary to affix a maker's mark to each piece. In France, only the king and his court were exempt from the royal ordinances governing the production and marking of silver: Louis XIV and Louis XV and members of their court are known to have commissioned silver for religious institutions in the colony, and these pieces did not always bear punch marks (Morisset, "L'orfèvrerie française," p. 27). At the Ursuline convent in Quebec City an unmarked ciborium is almost identical to No. 1 (Fox, "Liturgical Silver," fig. 2). Both ciboria may have been made by the same hand at about the same time, probably commissioned by a benevolent courtier or courtiers. One is at the oldest convent in New France, the Ursulines of Quebec City, founded in 1639, and the other at one of the oldest parish churches, Ange-Gardien, which dates from 1635 and received its first resident priest in 1667 (Magnan, p. 57).

ANONYMOUS, FRANCE (PARIS?)

2 Chalice, ca. 1675

MEASUREMENTS
Height 27.4 cm. (10¾ in.); diameter of cup 9.5 cm. (3¾ in.); diameter of base 16.4 cm. (6⁷⁄₁₆ in.); weight 547 gm. (17 oz. 12 dwt.)

MARK
FR in double oriflamme cartouche (stamped twice under foot)

CONDITION
Cup replaced in twentieth century

PROVENANCE
Church of Saint-Michel d'Yamaska, Yamaska County, Que.; Jean Octeau, Montreal; DIA purchase 29 July 1969.

BIBLIOGRAPHY
Recorded in church inventories of 1841 and 1864 and photographed by Gérard Morisset 22 September 1940 (see IBC, Yamaska file, photo C-2); *BDIA* 48 (1969):41 (ill.); Fox, "Liturgical Silver," pp. 102–3, fig. 6; Fox, "French Canadian Silver," pp. 78–79, fig. 3; Fox, *Traditional Arts,* no. 35.

EXHIBITIONS
Grosse Pointe Woods 1975; Windsor 1975

Gift of Mrs. Allan Shelden in memory of Robert H. Tannahill (acc. no. 69.172)

DESCRIPTION
Chalice consists of cup, stem, and foot screwed together by threaded connectors, similar to previous ciborium. The cup is bell-shaped with flared lip, gilt interior, and applied disc and threaded rod underneath. The baluster stem has an upper cylinder (threaded internally), bead and reel collar knop, two-part spool with applied beaded mid-molding, disc, urn-shaped knop, beaded band, raying collar, and lower bead and reel collar knop. The raised knop is ornamented with three winged angel heads and petaled bottom fringe. The angel heads were cast separately and then applied; the remaining ornament is embossed and chased. Each collar knop is a flange with applied band, worked with files to create a bead and reel; the beaded bands are similarly fashioned. The upper cylinder is swaged and seamed, the spool raised in two halves and the raying collar cast. All these elements are brazed together except the lower collar knop, which is brazed to the projecting cylinder of the foot. This knop contains a threaded sleeve which receives the projecting threaded rod of the adjacent rayed collar, joining the stem and foot. The foot is domed and splayed; a small cross on a hillock is engraved on the upper dome, which has a narrow everted edge. A punched and chased egg and dart flange is applied to the edge; below is an openwork acanthus border. Stamped and then cut, the leaves of the border are bound at their tips by an applied strengthening band.

As with ciboria, the interior of the chalice is always gilt because it holds the consecrated wine of the Mass. This chalice has an extreme flare to the lip which is more typical of the nineteenth century than of the seventeenth. That it is a replacement is confirmed by the elemental analysis, which indicates a silver differential of almost 4 percent between the cup and the remainder of the chalice, the latter having the higher readings. The foot and stem, at 96.44 percent and 97.15 percent, are within the Paris standard; the cup, at 92.57 percent, conforms to the sterling standard of 92.5 percent which has been enforced in Canada since 13 March 1908 (Tardy, p. 92). The absence of gold and lead traces in the cup also suggests that it is a relatively recent replacement (see Appendix II).

No. 2 was attributed to François Ranvoyzé, like No. 1, on the basis of the maker's mark, FR, which is probably a recent forgery (fig. 2). Ranvoyzé's career extended over a period of fifty years, and he used numerous marks, of which about twelve have been recorded, but the mark on this chalice is an unprecedented variant. The attribution was given credibility by the fact that he made a similar chalice for the church of Notre-Dame-de-Bonsecours, L'Islet, in 1810. The L'Islet chalice is a close reproduction of another at the same church by an anonymous French maker, dated 1700–1701 (*Ranvoyzé,* nos. 26 and 27 [ill.]). However, Ranvoyzé neglected to copy the bead and reel collar knops of the French piece, which are also found on the Detroit chalice, and this motif does not appear on any of his known ciboria and chalices. The overall execution of the Ranvoyzé chalice lacks the fineness of the French prototype, which closely resembles No. 2. Ranvoyzé made other chalices of related design, but they all possess the same awkward, provincial, almost naive character, and it should also be noted that he repeated several basic types of applied winged angel heads on numerous occasions and that these differ slightly from those of No. 2. The design of this piece is not found in the repertories of other Quebec silversmiths except Ignace-François Delezenne (ca. 1717–1790), in a chalice at the church of Notre-Dame-de-Foy, near Quebec City. However, Delezenne's treatment of the details is quite different (Trudel, no. 80 [ill.]).

The silver content of this chalice is within the Paris standard, but Ranvoyzé and other early Quebec silversmiths also worked within that standard (Meyers and Hanlan, p. 28). When Gérard Morisset photographed it in 1940 he noted that it was French, and the curé at Saint-Michel has recently stated that there had been, until recently, two chalices similar to the Detroit piece at his church, both French (letter of G. Farleyleuré to the author). The chalice photographed by Morisset is identical with No. 2, and Jean Octeau, the dealer, indicates that it came from Saint-Michel. The whereabouts of the other chalice are not known. The church was founded in 1727 (Magnan, p. 590); both chalices are probably the two recorded in the church inventories of 1841 and 1864 (IBC, Yamaska file).

The style of this chalice is early Louis XIV; many similar designs entered New France from about 1670 to 1710. In the earliest examples of this type, the holes of the basal openwork border are quite large, but they gradually diminish in size until about 1700, when the border is usually a solid frieze. On this basis No. 2 would date between 1670 and 1690.

No. 2 reproduces in almost every detail a chalice at Hôtel-Dieu, Quebec City (IBC, Hôtel-Dieu de Québec file, photo D-3). Attributed to Claude Ballin (1615–1678) of Paris, it bears the guild-warden's mark for the year 1673–74. The maker's mark consists of a crown, fleur-de-lis, two pellets, and the initials CB with a cluster of grapes. The finest details of these two chalices are identical: the acanthus leaves of the basal frieze, the engraved cross on the dome of the foot, and the angel heads on the knop—in fact, the heads seem to have been cast from the same mold. The

Fig. 2

only noticeable difference is in the lower leaf frieze of the knops. Both friezes consist of a large leaf alternating with a small leaf, but in No. 2 a small leaf is located directly under each winged angel head, whereas on the Hôtel-Dieu chalice a large leaf is in that spot.

Claude Ballin was the most illustrious French silversmith of the seventeenth century. He was Silversmith in Ordinary to King Louis XIV and Keeper of the Royal Mint. Although he was responsible for many important royal commissions, none of his work is known to survive in France today. Several other pieces of church silver in Quebec collections are attributed to him (Trudel, nos. 21, 22 [ill.]; Barbeau, *Trésor,* p. 73), all bearing the maker's mark mentioned above. If the Detroit chalice was fashioned by Ballin, it would have been a modest undertaking for such an important silversmith; it may very possibly be a product of his workshop.

3 Plate, ca. 1750

MEASUREMENTS
Height 2.8 cm. (1⅛ in.); diameter 28.9 cm. (11⅜ in.); weight 833.8 gm. (26 oz. 16 dwt.)

MARK
PL under fleur-de-lis and above five-pointed star, in shaped cartouche (stamped twice under rim)

INSCRIPTIONS
Engraved under bottom, GUY; scratched under rim, "cette assiette appartient Pierre Leduc" ("this plate belongs to Pierre Leduc")
Engraved on rim, arms of Godefroy de Tonnancour in crowned scroll and foliate cartouche (Massicotte and Roy, p. 136)

CONDITION
Small repair and some scraping under rim

PROVENANCE
Made for Louis-Joseph Godefroy de Tonnancour (1712–1784), Trois-Rivières, Que.; collection Guy family, Montreal; collection Pierre Leduc; Jean Octeau, Montreal; DIA purchase 10 February 1971.

Gift of Mrs. Allan Shelden in memory of her grandson, Allan Shelden IV (acc. no. 71.34)

DESCRIPTION
Flat circular bottom of plate curves shallowly to slightly convex five-scalloped rim with molded edge, fashioned by sinking or stretching with hammer. Molding applied in strips joined at the indented junctures of the scallops.

Fig. 3

The maker's mark on this plate, previously attributed to Paul Lambert dit Saint-Paul (1691 or 1703–1749), is highly suspect. Lambert is known to have used two marks, both very similar, which appear on about one hundred pieces authenticated by experts in the past (see fig. 39; Derome, p. 95 [ill.]). The mark on this plate deviates considerably from the two recognized variants, especially in the treatment of the fleur-de-lis, which is not a typical eighteenth-century rendition (fig. 3). The usual fleur-de-lis has three separate floral segments linked by a lower transverse bar; here they are rendered as a single unit. The cartouche framing the

Fig. 4. Attributed to Jean-François Landron, mark on plate. Detroit Institute of Arts, acc. no. 72.223.

26

No. 3

initials and devices is also too large and too symmetrical. This mark was first recognized about 1969, coincident with a rash of forgeries (see No. 2). Another suspect mark, attributed to Jean-François Landron (1686–ca. 1760), has the same faulty fleur-de-lis (fig. 4). Because actual forgeries are difficult to prove (see Appendix II), both of these marks are best dismissed as extremely doubtful.

The attribution of this plate to Lambert can be rejected on stylistic grounds as well. Lambert worked in a provincial northern French variation of the Louis XIV style, and nothing comparable to this Rococo plate is found in his oeuvre. The Rococo scallop design is typical of mid-eighteenth-century Parisian workshops. Indications of tampering where one would expect to find the punch marks on a French piece are also suspicious. For example, there is a highly burnished area under the rim, suggesting that marks have been erased. A repaired patch under the rim has a silver reading of 99.3 percent, indicating that it might have been electroplated in an attempt to disguise the removal of French marks (see Appendix II). The superb engraving also suggests a possible Parisian source, as does the silver content, which is apparently about 94.8 percent, within the range of the Paris standard.

This plate was part of a service, other pieces of which survive. All pieces were made in Paris, two items by Paul Soulaine, including a bowl of 1744–50 in the John L. Russell Collection (Trudel, no. 59 [ill.]) and a large plate of 1748 formerly in the McConnell Collection (DIA, *French in America,* no. 95). Another plate of 1752 was made by Nicolas-Clément Vallières of Paris (Trudel, no. 63 [ill.]). A silver service was an expensive undertaking, and it was not unusual for a Canadian gentleman-bourgeois to commission separate pieces over a period of time or from different workshops. The wealthy also preferred ordering from Paris to supporting the colonial silversmith. No. 3 is remarkably similar to these pieces in quality. Microscopic examination does reveal slight differences, however, in the engraved arms, and it may be from another Parisian workshop.

The original owner, Louis-Joseph Godefroy de Tonnancour, was a king's counsel and sub-delegate of the intendant of New France for the government of Trois-Rivières. He amassed a fortune in the fur trade and as a supplier of merchandise to the state, had extensive seigneurial estates (fiefs), and by the middle of the eighteenth century was one of the wealthiest men in Canada. His grandfather was ennobled in 1668, and the Tonnancour title was confirmed by Louis XIV, although not officially proclaimed until March 1718. On 11 May 1718, the Tonnancour arms were enregistered by Charles d'Hozier, juge d'armes et garde de l'armorial général de France.

On 11 February 1740 Louis-Joseph married Mary-Ann Seaman at Trois-Rivières. She was a native of New England but as a child had been abducted by the Abnaki Indians and brought to Trois-Rivières. Their eldest daughter, Marie, had as godfather Pierre de Rigaud, Marquis de Vaudreuil-Cavagnal, a governor of Louisiana and governor-general of New France from 1752 to 1760. Louis-Joseph married a second time in 1749; his wife, Louise, was the daughter of Pierre-André Carrerot, king's storekeeper and commissary-director of Ile Royale (Louisbourg) (Roy, *De Tonnancour,* pp. 51–57).

This plate, its companion (No. 4), and the bowl in the Russell Collection all came into the possession of the Guy family of Montreal, descendants of Pierre-Théodore Guy (1700-1748). The date is uncertain, but the inventory of the estate of Pierre-Théodore and his wife, Marianne Truillier, drawn up after the latter's death in 1770, lists four shaped plates and two shaped bowls among the silver (see Appendix I). The Russell bowl was transferred to the Bâby family of Montreal through the marriage of Élisabeth-Caroline Guy, great-granddaughter of Pierre-Théodore, to Joseph Bâby in 1831.

ANONYMOUS, FRANCE (PARIS?)

4 Plate, ca. 1750

MEASUREMENTS
Height 2.8 cm. (1⅛ in.); diameter 28.9 cm. (11⅜ in.); weight 833.1 gm. (26 oz. 16 dwt.)

MARK
PL under fleur-de-lis and above five-pointed star, in shaped cartouche (stamped twice under rim)

INSCRIPTIONS
Engraved under bottom, GUY
Engraved on rim, arms of Godefroy de Tonnancour in crowned scroll and foliate cartouche

CONDITION
Some scraping to rim

PROVENANCE
Made for Louis-Joseph Godefroy de Tonnancour, Trois-Rivières, Que.; collection Guy family, Montreal; Jean Octeau, Montreal; DIA purchase 26 February 1970.

EXHIBITIONS
Grosse Pointe Woods 1975

Robert H. Tannahill Fund and Robert H. Tannahill Memorial Fund (acc. no. 70.561)

DESCRIPTION
See No. 3

This plate is identical with No. 3, including the maker's mark and engraved arms, which are by the same left-handed engraver; both plates were probably made in the same workshop at about the same time. There is evidence of marks being removed here as well: the outer molding is gouged where the Paris mint contractor traditionally applied his discharge mark. Moreover, the so-called marks of Lambert appear to be machine-buffed to create the appearance of prolonged natural wear (fig. 5). The silver content of this plate is very high, ranging from 97.14 to 98.09 percent, above the Paris standard. At first these high readings suggested that the plate was electroplated, but analysis after polishing, sanding, and scraping the bottom produced the same results.

No. 4

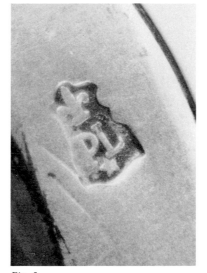

Fig. 5

ANONYMOUS, CANADA OR FRANCE

5 Cruet, ca. 1750–60

MEASUREMENTS
Height 9.5 cm. (3¾ in.); diameter of belly 4.7 cm. (1⅞ in.); diameter of base 4.4 cm. (1¾ in.); weight 103.7 gm. (3 oz. 7 dwt.)

INSCRIPTIONS
Engraved on lid, EAU ("water"); engraved under lid, SG; painted under foot, GM (Gérard Morisset)

CONDITION
Slight repairs to bottom of foot

PROVENANCE
Collection Louis Carrier, Sainte-Anne de Bellevue, Que.; collection Gérard Morisset, Quebec City; Jean Octeau, Montreal; DIA purchase 5 November 1969.

BIBLIOGRAPHY
Morisset, "Sculpture," p. 39 (ill.); Morisset, "XVIIIe siècle," p. 16, fig. 3; *BDIA* 48 (1969):42 (ill.).

Gift of Mr. and Mrs. Allan Shelden III (acc. no. 69.265)

DESCRIPTION
Raised pear-form body with shaped lip, flared at back by handle joining and drawn to short spout at front. A highly burnished neck curves to a bulbous paunch with a shaped frieze of lightly embossed naturalistic marsh flora, on a matte and punched ground, of cattails alternating with small rush-like and floral clumps. It has a curved front lid with a three-part pinned hinge and a segmental back-plate which is brazed to the cruet's lip. A handle in a fluted harp shape of reverse scrolls, brazed at the back-plate and the upper paunch, has a lower terminal of a free-floating scroll tip. A circular domed foot with gadrooned border has an applied outer strengthening band and is brazed to the bottom of the body. All sections are fashioned by hammering except the cast handle.

The marsh flora on the body of this cruet indicate its function as a water container. Originally it may have had a mate which contained wine (see No. 9). This piece was previously ascribed to Paul Lambert of Quebec City, but we now know that it cannot be Lambert's. His only two known cruets, an identical pair made for the church of Notre-Dame-de-Lorette, Village-des-Hurons, near Quebec City (fig. 6), are robust and heavy in proportions, abstract in decorative patterning, and have extensive punching, gadrooning, and reeding, all characteristic of Lambert, who usually worked in a provincial northern French variation of

Fig. 6. Paul Lambert dit Saint-Paul, two cruets, H.15.5 cm. Church of Notre-Dame-de-Lorette, Village-des-Hurons, Quebec.

the Louis XIV style. The Detroit cruet is delicate and sophisticated in its diminutive proportions, contrasting textures, naturalistic foliage, and scrolled counter-curves. These are all characteristics of the Rococo style, which never made any real inroads in the early silver of Canada; furthermore, Rococo designs were not commonly used for church vessels in France until after 1750. In the first half of the eighteenth century, French ecclesiastical plate was almost always fashioned in a sober late Louis XIV style (there were a few exceptions in the Rococo style, but these were usually the work of Parisian silversmiths).

The silver content of this cruet ranges from 93.82 to 93.86 percent and is therefore below the Paris standard (see Appendix II). The silver reading suggests that it was made either in New France or in the French provinces. While most provinces followed the Paris standard, a few, such as the Franche-Comté, Hainault, and Flanders, had their own. Flanders' standard was 94.44 percent with an allowance of 0.694 percent, within the range of No. 5 (Carré, pp. 5–6). However, the silver reading points to New France as a more probable source, but this Rococo cruet has no stylistic equivalent in the oeuvre of any eighteenth-century Quebec silversmith and cannot at present be attributed to a particular maker.

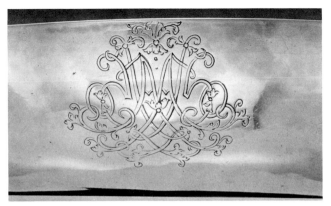

Fig. 7

ANONYMOUS, QUEBEC OR DETROIT

6 Écuelle, ca. 1725–50

MEASUREMENTS
Height 4.1 cm. (1⅝ in.); diameter 16.7 cm. (6⁹⁄₁₆ in.); length 28 cm. (11 in.); weight 407.6 gm. (13 oz. 2 dwt.)

INSCRIPTIONS
Engraved cipher on side of bowl (fig. 7), AL; stamped letters outside rim, DRL

CONDITION
Small repairs on rim by each handle

PROVENANCE
Collection Moran (originally Morand) family, Detroit—earliest known owner Charles Moran (1797–1876), but may have belonged to his grandfather, Claude-Charles Morand (1722–1755) (FWR); gift to DIA of grandson of Charles Moran 2 December 1957.

BIBLIOGRAPHY
Robinson, ''Early Detroit,'' p. 5; Fox, ''French Canadian Silver,'' p. 78, fig. 2; Fox, *Traditional Arts,* no. 37.

EXHIBITIONS
Windsor 1975

Gift of J. Bell Moran (acc. no. 57.220)

DESCRIPTION
Low raised bowl with slightly convex bottom and two symmetrically opposed earlug handles. The handles are cut from a flat piece of silver to which a precast palmette or shell motif is riveted. A small thickening bracket is applied underneath each handle to strengthen the joining with the bowl.

A popular and traditional French vessel, the écuelle is a low two-handled soup bowl. While most écuelles produced in France had a cover, and, in the eighteenth century, a plate, those in the colony often lacked these accessories. The appearance in Quebec of the écuelle without cover or plate was a provincial variation spawned by a shortage of silver rather than any change in taste. This design, with handles of schematized triangular outline and applied shell, dates from the late seventeenth and early eighteenth centuries in France but was popular as late as the mid-eighteenth century in Quebec.

This écuelle is the work of a skilled craftsman and could have been produced in Detroit by such silversmiths as Jean-Baptiste Baudry dit des Buttes dit Saint-Martin (1684–1755), Pierre Belleperche (1699–1767), or Pierre Barthe (1733–1763+). While the silversmithing activities of Baudry and Barthe are somewhat obscure, Belleperche was making silver at Quebec City before 1720. On 2 May 1715 he began a three-year apprenticeship under Jean-Baptiste Soullard (ca. 1677–ca. 1720), who taught him the craft of gunsmith as well as silversmith (Derome, p. 21). Belleperche settled in Detroit sometime prior to 17 September 1725. At the birth of his daughter Angélique in Detroit on 9 Feburary 1728 he was referred to as ''gunsmith of the fort [Detroit],'' and at the marriage of his daughter Françoise to Joseph Pouget on 22 January 1759 he was called a ''master gunsmith,'' suggesting that this was his chief occupation (BHC, RBMB, Sainte Anne, Detroit). His work with silver at Detroit was probably limited to minor repairs, although he was quite capable of producing silver wares such as écuelles. However, the excellence of the engraved cipher on this piece, unless added later, suggests it was made in Quebec. It was possibly brought to Detroit by Claude-Charles Morand, who settled there about 1749. The dimensions as well as the design are almost identical with those of an écuelle by the enigmatic ''LV'' of Montreal about 1750 (Trudel, no. 133 [ill.]). But the daughter of Pierre Belleperche, Marie-Anne, married Claude-Charles Morand at Sainte Anne's Church, Detroit, on 22 September 1751 (BHC). Thus the Moran owners of this piece were descendants of the silversmith-gunsmith Belleperche.

Laurent Amiot (Amyot)

Quebec City

1764–1839

Born at Quebec City on 1 August 1764, Laurent was the son of Jean Amiot, a prosperous merchant and tavernkeeper, and Marie-Louise Chrétien. He may have learned the craft of silversmith from his brother, Jean-Nicolas, who served as an apprentice under Joseph Schindler, or from François Ranvoyzé. About 1783 he was sent to Paris for further training by the priests of the Séminaire de Québec, in the company of abbé Germain du Devant (Langdon, *Canadian Silversmiths,* pp. 40–41). He must have been trained in one of the better Parisian workshops, for he returned to Quebec City in 1787 skilled in the latest Parisian designs and techniques. His influence on the silversmiths of Quebec City was immediate and overwhelming. Even the outstanding silversmith François Ranvoyzé was not spared, as outmoded Louis XIV liturgical designs were supplanted by the Louis XVI style. Amiot also introduced new Parisian silversmithing techniques, such as a greater use of casting, which made production faster and more efficient and foreshadowed the technological developments of the later nineteenth-century silver manufacturers.

Amiot's first workshop was located at 2 Côte de la Montagne; in the 1830s he was at 1 rue Saint-Pierre (*ibid.*). On 1 February 1792, Paul Morin was apprenticed to him for five years (ANQQ, Charles Voyer minutes). The following year, on 9 April, Amiot married Marguerite Levasseur Borgia (ANQQ, RBMB, Notre-Dame de Québec). In 1817 he was a churchwarden at Notre-Dame Basilica. Two later apprentices were François Sasseville, who became his companion and eventually his successor, and Pierre Lespérance. Amiot died on 3 June 1839 (Morisset, ''Sasseville,'' pp. 51–52).

In quality and quantity of production, Amiot was the most important Quebec silversmith from about 1790 until his death. His success was largely due to his ecclesiastical sponsorship, which was translated into church commissions. The clergy of the Quebec City region clearly preferred the more contemporary French designs of Amiot, and other local silversmiths were compelled to follow suit. After 1800, as his influence gradually became felt in the Montreal region, his designs, or derivatives thereof, were sometimes adopted by silversmiths such as Pierre Huguet dit Latour. His success also extended to domestic silver, where he proved adept at working in the English Neoclassic style. Early in his career he executed a few superb pieces in the Louis XVI style (see the ewer at the Archevêché de Québec, in Langdon, *Canadian Silversmiths,* pl. 28), and he occasionally achieved a unique synthesis of Louis XVI and English Rococo design elements, as in the Bâby tureen (*ibid.,* pl. 49). Toward the end of his fifty-year career, Amiot experimented with the more current Neo-Rococo style (Ignatieff, p. 151 [ill.]), but his domestic production is predominantly of English Neoclassic inspiration.

LAURENT AMIOT

7 Ciborium, ca. 1800–1810

MEASUREMENTS
Height 25.6 cm (10 1/16 in.); diameter of bowl 11.5 cm. (4 1/2 in.); diameter of base 12.5 cm. (4 15/16 in.); weight 750.3 gm. (24 oz. 2 dwt.)

MARK
LA in oval (stamped once under foot)

CONDITION
Threaded rod of bowl replaced

PROVENANCE
Reportedly church of Saint-Thomas de Montmagny, Montmagny County, Que.; Jean Octeau, Montreal; DIA purchase 12 December 1969.

BIBLIOGRAPHY
BDIA 48 (1969):36 (ill.); Fox, ''Liturgical Silver,'' p. 103.

Robert H. Tannahill Fund (acc. no. 69.297)

DESCRIPTION
Ciborium of five separable parts: cover, bowl, calyx, baluster stem, and foot. The cover is raised in a low central dome and curved outer shoulder, with an applied outer horizontal flange and a vertical seamed band forming the lip. A plain cross finial is riveted to the dome. The bowl has vertical sides with a rounded bottom edge and a slightly convex inside bottom. The bead applied below the rim forms a bezel, beneath which a gadrooned calyx envelops the bowl's exterior surface. The interiors of the bowl and cover are mercury-gilt. The baluster stem has an inverted pyriform knop and a lower secondary bell-form cushion knop with torus, both plain except for two small stepped moldings. A circular domed and splayed foot has a projecting stepped flange and outer cavetto molding. Elaborate chased and shallow fluted raying strapwork, with a matte scallop border, flares out from the lower stem and covers the upper dome, a type of strapwork characteristic of Amiot and also found on his Detroit chalice (No. 11).

The basic construction and methods used in fashioning this ciborium, with slight variations, are used in most ciboria and chalices made by Amiot and his successor, François Sasseville.

The cover, bowl, calyx, and bell form of the cushion knop were each fashioned by a combined process of annealing (heating) and raising (hammering) a flat disc of silver on an anvil. By varying the sizes and shapes of the anvils, stakes, and hammers used, many different shapes could be achieved. The calyx would then have been scored and the gadroons embossed and chased. The smaller segments of the stem—the upper spool, cylinder with applied bead, torus, rods, and sleeves, and the discs at the bottom of the bowl, top of the stem, step of the knop, and upper torus—were formed by swaging (shaping) and seaming flat pieces of silver. The foot was raised as a single unit, and then the lower half was cut away and swaged to create the cavetto molding. Other elements such as the lip of the cover, the basal flange, and the basal strengthening band were drawn. The cross finial was cut from a flat sheet of silver.

The method used in fashioning the knop is not so easily discerned. Traditionally it is raised; here it appears to have been cast and then turned; but even if actually raised, it still might have been turned. This final turning on a lathe slightly shapes, smoothes, and polishes the outer surface. Amiot could have learned the use of the lathe, as well as casting, during his Parisian apprenticeship, but all this is purely hypothetical; the techniques of Quebec silversmiths during this period require much further study.

To form each of the five larger sections of the ciborium, the appropriate elements were united by brazing where necessary. For example, in the foot the torus of the lower knop was brazed to the cylinder of the domed upper foot above the small fillet binding the strapwork. The domed and splayed elements were brazed together with the basal flange, and then the strengthening rim was applied. In a similar manner, the cover and stem were assembled.

The bowl, calyx, stem, and foot were finally assembled by means of two pairs of threaded rods and sleeves. A small disc and threaded rod are brazed to the bottom of the bowl, and a threaded cylinder or sleeve is inserted into a tapping hole at the top of the stem. The calyx has a small circular perforation at its center which fits over the rod of the bowl. Another rod projects from the bottom of the bell form of the lower knop and is tangent to a sleeve in the torus. Thus these four sections can be screwed together tightly to form a single unit which is also easily disassembled. Developed in the seventeenth century, this traditional French method of assembling ciboria and chalices was used in Quebec until the end of the nineteenth century.

This ciborium is one of several known examples by Amiot with a bowl set in a gadrooned calyx. Its overall design is restrained to the point of severity: the natural luster of the silver is enhanced through highly polished, relatively plain surfaces. This ciborium was influenced by the Neoclassic aesthetic of the Louis XVI style, very familiar to Amiot from his Parisian training. It probably dates from the early phase of his career, which is marked by restraint, refinement, and high quality. An early date is supported by the punch mark (fig. 8), or silversmith's identity mark, consisting of his initials. He used different marks throughout his career, as did many Quebec silversmiths: this one is identical with that found on his censer from Saint-Cuthbert (Berthier) of 1804 (fig. 10).

Another ciborium by Amiot at the church of Saint-Thomas de Montmagny is almost identical with the Detroit piece except that the calyx does not cover the entire bowl and has alternating long and short gadroons and the cross finial is more elaborate. Barbeau ("Deux cents ans," figs. 9, 18) also illustrates two other ciboria at this church, one by François Ranvoyzé, the other by François Sasseville. The parish of Saint-Thomas de Montmagny was founded in 1678 (Magnan, p. 700) and was quite populous by the beginning of the nineteenth century. The parish priest undoubtedly required extra ciboria, but it is questionable whether he needed four. No. 7 may in fact not come from this church. None of these vessels is recorded in the parish account books.

There is another almost identical ciborium by Amiot, at the National Gallery of Canada (fig. 9), and both represent one of the four or five standard designs he employed for ciboria. However, he sometimes worked in a more decorative Louis XVI style, such as in an example at the church of

Fig. 8

Fig. 9. Laurent Amiot, ciborium. H. 26 cm. National Gallery of Canada, Ottawa, acc. no. 16,859.

Saint-Louis, Lotbinière, dated about 1820 (Morisset, *Lotbinière*, pl. 23), in which the knop is an inverted and angular bell form, with a beaded molding and laurel leaf frieze, and the domed cover has a rosette surround with chased and fluted petals. This ornament has been integrated with adjacent plain surfaces, creating a rather handsome piece. His later works were not usually so successful; under the influence of the Empire style, they became overladen with surface decoration and the proportions grew heavier. A ciborium (No. 43) by François Sasseville, made about 1852, almost duplicates this one except for the absence of a calyx, and testifies to the persistent popularity of Amiot's formulas long after even Amiot himself had ceased to use them.

36

LAURENT AMIOT

8 Censer, 1804

MEASUREMENTS
Height 23 cm. (9 in.); diameter of burner 11.4 cm. (4½ n.); diameter of base 8.3 cm. (3¼ in.); weight 807.7 gm. (25 oz. 19 dwt.)

MARK
LA in oval (stamped twice under foot) (fig. 10)

CONDITION
Repairs to rings at upper rim of bowl and finial and replacement of terminal links of connecting chains; slightly worn spur openings and dented upper chimney

PROVENANCE
Church of Saint-Cuthbert, Berthier County, Que.; H. Baron, Montreal; DIA purchase 30 October 1957.

BIBLIOGRAPHY
IBC, Saint-Cuthbert (Berthier) file, photo B-5 (photographed by Gérard Morisset about 1940); *BDIA* 37 (1957–58):36 (ill.); DIA, *Tannahill*, p. 68; Fox, *Traditional Arts*, no. 44.

EXHIBITIONS
Windsor 1975

Gift of Robert H. Tannahill (acc. no. 57.145)

DESCRIPTION
Censer composed of footed bowl, two-tiered openwork cover or chimney, and finger-plate with four suspension chains. The raised, urn-shaped bowl is decorated with a lower frieze of fluted tongues with chased borders and three repoussé garlands on the shoulder. Each garland contains clusters of three laurel leaves with two berries except the lowest, where the berries vary from two to four. A small looped wire is riveted through an applied disc on the shoulder at the point of suspension of each garland, and one of three outer chains is attached to each. The mouth of the bowl has a bezel of an applied, drawn, and seamed band. The bowl serves as the burner section, but the charcoal and incense were actually burned in a cylindrical, flat-bottomed pan, or fire-pan, which fits into its mouth.

This unit is brazed to a splayed and molded foot fashioned in three segments: a raised trumpet form, a molded footband chased with double outlined beads, and an outer strengthening band. A raised two-tiered and bell-shaped chimney surmounts the burner bowl. In the lower tier three openwork panels are separated by three boldly projecting cast and applied consoles with spurs, each of which has an upper keyhole-shaped opening and extends out over one of three rings on the shoulder of the bowl. Each outer chain, attached to a ring, passes through a spur opening, linking the two main sections of the censer. Openwork panels in the form of a swirling sunburst with pierced and chased petals fan out from a small central oval boss.

Fig. 10

Fig. 11. Pierre Huguet dit Latour, censer. H. 23 cm. Formerly Paul Gouin Collection, Montreal.

The bell-shaped crowning tier of the cover has a lower torus molding chased with double outlined beads, as on the foot. The side of the bell is encircled by a frieze of vertical openwork with chased border functioning as ventilator holes. At the top, small embossed and chased gadroons surround a cast flame finial which is riveted through the cover. The finial has a small vent hole and ring to which the central chain is attached.

The entire vessel is suspended by four chains attached to the finger-plate, a plain disc with a convex center, applied outer band, and screwed ball finial with inserted ring. Three rings are brazed underneath the outer edge of the disc, to which the outer chains are attached, and there is a small hole for the central chain with a large terminal ring which allows the cover to be raised to add incense to the burner while the vessel is suspended.

In the early phase of Amiot's career, he was most influenced by the Louis XVI style. Although the two-tiered, bell-shaped cover with three openwork panels and three consoles with spurs and the bowl on a trumpet foot are typical of Louis XIV censers (Trudel, no. 53), the Louis

XIV trellis openwork is replaced here by the sunburst, and the squat and bulbous Louis XIV bowl is abandoned for the shape of a classical urn. Motifs such as the garlands of laurel leaves and the bead and tongue patterns are also in the Louis XVI style; whereas Louis XVI ornament was often cast and applied, Amiot preferred the embossing and (or) chasing of the earlier style. The relative chasteness and harmonious cohesion of the overall design is in accordance with the Louis XVI aesthetic. The vertical outline of the form is slightly emphasized, for a light and delicate effect which is both complemented and offset by the subtle horizontal accents of the plain and decorated bands. This censer is an exquisite example of Amiot's early work.

The book of minutes and the account books of the parish council of Saint-Cuthbert indicate the procedure for ordering liturgical vessels and their cost. The minutes of 18 September 1803 read: "Meeting of the retired and active churchwardens for the rendering of accounts; it was unanimously resolved that a sum of money of about 1,500 livres, or more, would be taken from the strongbox for a lamp, a censer with incense-boat, and a holy water stoup, all in silver" (IBC, Saint-Cuthbert [Berthier] file, Livre de délibérations, I [1787–1878]:20v–21r). Purchases of silver by a parish church were made by the council of three elected churchwardens, who, in fact, handled all the financial affairs of the church. When especially important financial decisions were made, they were usually joined by their predecessors, as indicated in the minutes quoted.

This council met again on 26 February 1804, and approved a contract with Laurent Amiot for the making of these pieces: "Meeting of the retired and active churchwardens: it has been concluded firstly that the contract of the silversmith was accepted, namely 50 louis for the lamp, 12 louis 10 shillings for the holy water stoup, and 20 louis for the censer, all in silver" (ibid., p. 21v). The council paid Amiot 1,200 livres for the sanctuary lamp the same year (ibid., Livre de comptes, I [1798–1880]). As the number of livres per louis fluctuated slightly, this transaction supplies the current rate of exchange. The louis was worth 24 livres; therefore, the initial valuation of the censer and incense-boat was 480 livres. Such a considerable amount of money was customarily paid in installments. Accordingly, in 1805 two payments were made on the holy water stoup and censer with incense-boat, one of 443 livres 7 sols, the other of 268 livres 18 sols. In 1806 a final payment of 93 livres was made on the censer. The total cost of the three pieces was 805 livres 5 sols. The final cost of the censer and incense-boat was actually slightly more than the initial valuation, almost 500 livres. The value of the censer alone is difficult to calculate, as it was purchased with the incense-boat as a set (the present whereabouts of the incense-boat is not known).

The council later purchased another censer from Pierre Huguet of Montreal (Morisset, *Évolution*, pl. 17); as recorded in the first account book in 1812, it cost 528 livres. This censer was undoubtedly inspired by Amiot's, but its execution is less successful, it is somewhat awkward, and Huguet used the bright-cut technique on the garlands of the bowl in place of the lightly embossed garlands of Amiot. While it is recognized that Huguet sometimes borrowed designs from Amiot, as did other Quebec silversmiths of this period, this censer may indicate a specific borrowing. He employed this design in many of his censers and especially liked the swirling sunburst of the chimney (fig. 11). While Amiot handled this motif especially skillfully in the Detroit censer, he repeats it rarely, usually preferring a sunburst with straight petals spreading out in a symmetrical fashion (No. 10).

9 Pair of Cruets and Tray, ca. 1825

MEASUREMENTS
Cruets: height 13 cm. (5⅛ in.); diameter of belly 5.9 cm. (2 5/16 in.); diameter of base 5.1 cm. (2 in.); weight of left cruet 192.6 gm. (6 oz. 2 dwt.); weight of right cruet 192.4 gm. (6 oz. 2 dwt.). *Tray:* height 1.8 cm. (11/16 in.); length 19.1 cm. (7½ in.); width 13.7 cm. (5⅜ in.); weight 210.6 gm. (6 oz. 15 dwt.)

MARK
LA in oval (stamped twice under foot of each cruet and three times under tray)

INSCRIPTIONS
Stamped on outer basal rim of cruets, ST: ANT.D.T. (Saint-Antoine de Tilly); engraved on body of one cruet, A (*aqua*); engraved on body of other cruet, V (*vinum*).

PROVENANCE
Church of Saint-Antoine de Tilly, Lotbinière County, Que.; H. Baron, Montreal; DIA purchase 5 October 1953.

BIBLIOGRAPHY
IBC, Saint-Antoine de Tilly file, photos A-9 and A-10 (photographed by Gérard Morisset 30 August 1943); *Art Quarterly* 17 (1954):70; *Canadian Art* 40 (1954):157; *BDIA* 33 (1954):78 (ill.); Greening, fig. 3; DIA, *Tannahill,* pp. 68–69 (ill.); Fox, *Traditional Arts,* no. 45.

EXHIBITIONS
Windsor 1975

Gift of Robert H. Tannahill (acc. no. 53.320 a, b, c)

DESCRIPTION
Each cruet has a pear form body, elongated pinched neck, and shaped rim with long beak-like spout. Decoration is limited to an applied and molded neck band and a molded lip with scroll back. The bodies are composed of two raised sections seamed at the neck band; the feet have three brazed sections, a swaged rim band and molding and a raised trumpet form. The oval tray has a raised and everted rim with applied molding.

Fig. 12.   *Laurent Amiot, cruets. Private collection.*

Originally each cruet may have had a stopper, a cork with a silver ring. The only distinguishing feature of these vessels is the large engraved ''A'' and ''V'' to indicate their respective functions as receptacles for the water and wine used both in the Eucharist and in ceremonial lustrations during the Mass. Such cruet sets usually include a tray. Laurent Amiot made two cruet sets for the church of Saint-Antoine de Tilly, and they are remarkably similar in design. The only difference is the slightly greater height and more elaborate foot of the Detroit pair and the tray of the second set, which is deeper and raised on a molded and splayed footband and may also have been used as a lavabo, or basin, for the ritual washings during the Mass. Over all, restraint and simplicity characterizes these minor but important liturgical vessels.

Because of constant use, cruets such as these frequently became disfigured—their life expectancy was even shorter than that of a censer. For this reason Amiot utilized two standard, but similar, designs. The Detroit cruets, with their tall pear-form bodies, represent one type; the other (fig. 12) has a plain urn-shaped body, a trumpet foot, and diminutive overall proportions. These formulas were repeated throughout Amiot's later career, were adopted by many of his contemporaries, and persisted even into the late nineteenth century. A notable example of his influence can be seen as late as 1876 in a pair of cruets by Pierre Lespérance (1819–1882) for the church of Saint-Famille, Cap-Santé (Morisset, *Cap-Santé,* pl. 23). Except for the mark of the silversmith, they are indistinguishable from No. 9 here.

The standardization of design renders the dating of these pieces on the basis of style virtually impossible. However, Amiot's mark on the Detroit cruets (fig. 13) and tray (fig. 14) is identical with that found on his chalice and incense-boat from Saint-Jean-Chrysostome, Lévis County, and dating from the 1830s (see figs. 16 and 17), suggesting a later date for these pieces. Their original cost was probably about 12 louis, a sum paid for a similar cruet set at Saint-Jean-Chrysostome in 1837 (IBC, Saint-Jean-Chrysostome [Lévis] file, Livre de comptes, I [1829–71]:36).

Fig. 13

Fig. 14

No. 9

10 Censer, ca. 1825

MEASUREMENTS
Height 27.1 cm. (11$\frac{11}{16}$ in); diameter of burner 13.3 cm. (5$\frac{1}{4}$ in.); diameter of base 9.2 cm. (3$\frac{5}{8}$ in.); weight, 1,190.8 gm. (38 oz. 5 dwt.)

MARK
LA in oval (stamped four times under foot)

PROVENANCE
Private collection, Toronto, Ont.; S. Breitman Antiques Ltd., Westmount (Montreal); DIA purchase 10 February 1971.

BIBLIOGRAPHY
Fox, "French Canadian Silver," p. 79, fig. 4.

Miscellaneous Gifts Fund (acc. no. 71.33)

DESCRIPTION
Footed bowl with fire-pan, chimney cover, and finger-plate with four suspension chains, made like No. 8 but with slight variations. The shoulder of the urn-shaped bowl has alternating long and short chased gadroons, the long gadroons having a second chased outline and the entire frieze a chased scallop border. The lower bowl has a frieze of fluted tongues with raised and chased edges and a chased scallop border. The foot is composed of three brazed sections: a drawn and seamed rim band, wrought and chased gadrooned molding, and a raised trumpet form. Covering the bowl is a two-tiered chimney through which the aromatic fumes rise. The lower tier has three openwork panels in the form of a sunburst with flaring pierced rays and a central quatrefoil. Each openwork panel is separated by a projecting console with a spur; each spur contains a cylindrical insert which fits over a ring with an attached chain on the shoulder of the bowl. The bell-shaped upper tier has a gadrooned torus and sides with a tripartite openwork frieze of groupings of four ventilator holes, each grouping flanked by flat chased scrolls which radiate out from top. The top of the bell has a petaled surround, and the entire censer is crowned by a cast bud finial with a vent hole and small ring to which the central chain is attached. The slightly concave disc, serving as a finger-plate, has a chased quatrefoil motif, a brazed ring finial containing a large suspension ring, and a chain hole with applied strengthening rim.

Amiot rarely made two censers exactly alike, and particular preferences in decoration and proportions can sometimes be associated with different phases of his career. For example, this censer has a slight overabundance of decoration characteristic of his later work; the openwork panels of the chim-

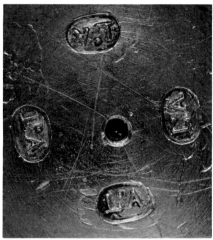

Fig. 15

ney are more complex; the pierced rays of the sunbursts are partially stopped; and the shoulder of the bowl is gadrooned with especially prominent bosses. The proportions of this censer were also a later preference of Amiot. The burner's shoulder has been slightly extended, and the overall effect is somewhat ponderous in contrast to the well-proportioned designs of his early censers (No. 8).

This censer is very similar to examples by Amiot at the churches of Sainte-Famille (Ile d'Orléans) and Saint-Jean-Chrysostome (Lévis). These are dated 1835 and 1837, respectively, and the cost of each (with an incense-boat) was 600 livres or 25 louis (IBC, Sainte-Famille [Ile d'Orléans] file, photo 16–21, and Saint-Jean-Chrysostome [Lévis] file, photo B-1). The punch mark, which appears to be one used by Amiot later in his career (fig. 15), is identical with the mark on a chalice which he made for the church of Saint-Jean-Chrysostome (Lévis) about 1828–37 (see fig. 16).

LAURENT AMIOT

11 Chalice, 1828–37

MEASUREMENTS
Height 25.1 cm. (9⅞ in.); diameter of cup 9.1 cm. (3⁹⁄₁₆ in.); diameter of base 15 cm. (5⅞ in.); weight 745.9 gm. (24 oz. 1 dwt.)

MARK
LA in oval (stamped twice under foot)

PROVENANCE
Church of Saint-Jean-Chrysostome, Lévis County, Que.; sold 1958–60 (according to sacristan); Jean Octeau, Montreal; DIA purchase 4 November 1970.

BIBLIOGRAPHY
Fox, *Traditional Arts,* no. 46 (ill.).

EXHIBITIONS
Windsor 1975

Elizabeth, Allan, and Warren Shelden Fund (acc. no. 70.834)

DESCRIPTION
Four separable parts screwed together with threaded cylinders and fashioned like Amiot's ciborium (see No. 7): a cup, a calyx, a stem, and a foot. The parcel, or partially gilt, interior and exterior half of the cup are mercury-gilt; the remainder retains the natural luster of silver.

The raised, bell-shaped cup, with a flared lip, has its lower half encased in a calyx of alternating long and short gadroons with intervening bands, extended in an openwork scallop above each long gadroon. The scallops are linked by horizontal bars, creating an openwork border for the calyx.

The baluster stem has an upper spool, a disc forming a step, an urn-shaped knop, a small cylinder with applied bead, and a lower bell form. The knop, which in this instance is definitely raised, has a chased band of gadrooning on the shoulder, a plain mid-band, and a lower frieze consisting of flutes with raised and chased borders, alternating with chased vertical bands incised with a triple arrow and dot motif. The lower stem has a torus cushion knop with an upper and a lower disc and chased with an alternating bead and oval motif, and a flared cylinder; this section is brazed to the foot, and a molded band is applied to the joining.

The domed and splayed foot has a dentiled flange projecting over a cavetto molding and an outer strengthening band. There is a small engraved cross, as on most chalices, above the flange. Elaborate chased and shallow fluted raying strapwork, with a matte scallop border, flares out from the lower stem and over the upper dome.

The complex decoration of this chalice is more typical of Amiot's later work, as is the technique of exterior gilding, which did not come into popular usage in Quebec until the second quarter of the nineteenth century. Height has been reduced by eliminating the upper collar knop, resulting in a proportionally larger foot and central knop in the overall design. This aspect contrasts markedly with another chalice by Amiot at the church of Sainte-Famille, Cap-Santé, dated 1801 (Morisset, *Cap-Santé,* pl. 18), which, while almost identical in design, is taller, has the usual three knops, and exemplifies the slender and graceful proportions which Amiot borrowed from the Louis XVI style. A late date is further supported by the maker's mark (fig. 16), which is identical with that on an incense-boat made by Amiot for the same church in 1837 (see fig. 17). The parish of Saint-Jean-Chrysostome was not founded until 1828 (Magnan, p. 467); therefore this chalice was commissioned some time between that year and 1839. While there is no direct reference to this chalice in the first parish account book, an entry for 1832 reads: "Various articles from Mr. Amiot, 190 livres, 2 sols" (IBC, Saint-Jean-Chrysostome [Lévis] file, Livre de comptes, I [1829–71]). However, this payment could be no more than an installment, as a chalice would usually cost at least twice that sum.

From 1834 until 1837 there are numerous other references to Laurent Amiot in the first parish account book. The following purchases are recorded: in 1834, ampullae (vials for holy oils) for 2 louis, 12 shillings, 9 pence; in 1835, a chrismatory with three ampullae for 6 louis; in 1837, a pair of cruets with tray for 12 louis and a pyx for 3 louis (*ibid.,* pp. 26, 29, 31, 36, 37). Apparently the most important silver acquisitions made prior to 1837 were not recorded; thus the omission of the Detroit chalice is not strange. On 14 June 1837, Mgr Signay, bishop of Quebec, reprimanded the churchwardens for failing to list several purchases of silver in their expenditures for that year, among them a censer and the incense-boat shown in No. 12, both by Laurent Amiot, and the third piece, a monstrance, was probably made by him as well (*ibid.,* p. 31), as all the surviving Quebec silver at this church bears his mark.

The only other extant silver from Saint-Jean-Chrysostome consists of several nineteenth-century pieces imported from France. Following the restoration of the French monarchy in 1814, French liturgical silver was again imported into Quebec. The imports began as a trickle but by the late 1830s posed a real threat to Quebec silversmiths, who, in response, began to adopt the more current designs and techniques of their French competitors. Amiot's use of exterior gilding on some of his later pieces, like this chalice, is an example of such a response.

Fig. 16

No. 11

LAURENT AMIOT

12 Incense-boat, ca. 1837

MEASUREMENTS
Height 10.6 cm. (4$\frac{3}{16}$ in.); length of boat 13.5 cm. (5$\frac{5}{16}$ in.); length of base 7.6 cm. (3 in.); weight 240.8 gm. (7 oz. 15 dwt.)

MARK
LA in oval (stamped three times under foot) (fig. 17)

PROVENANCE
Church of Saint-Jean-Chrysostome, Lévis County, Que.; sold 1958–60 (according to sacristan); Roger Prévost, Quebec City; Jean Octeau, Montreal; DIA purchase 11 July 1968.

BIBLIOGRAPHY
IBC, Saint-Jean-Chrysostome (Lévis) file, photo B-1 (photographed by Gérard Morriset, September 1939); Fox, *Traditional Arts,* no. 47.

EXHIBITIONS
Windsor 1975

Gift of Mr. and Mrs. Allan Shelden III (acc. no. 68.161)

DESCRIPTION
Boat-shaped incense receptacle with lip or pouring spout rising in a tapered curve, supported on a raised splayed and oval foot with applied stepped band and rim, the body of boat raised and lip drawn. The dominant motif is a petal-like shallow flute or tongue with a raised matte edge, a central circle and dot, and a chased double outline, repeated around the entire boat except at the very bottom, which has an embossed petaled surround; the scallops of the tongues are tangent to a plain banded rim with shaped and applied molding.

The cover has two sections, a fixed back-plate and a hinged front with a five-part pinned hinge. All ornament is embossed and chased in low relief. The front section has an applied outer molding and a shaped reserve containing a trilobed leaf flanked by two scrolls at the hinged end, two flanking scrolls by the spout, and C-shellwork on the central portion, all on a punched ground. The outer molding, the two scrolls with the leaf, and the shellwork are all repeated on the back-plate.

Acquired in 1837 or slightly earlier along with a censer for 25 louis (IBC, Saint-Jean-Chrysostome [Lévis] file, Livre de comptes, I [1829–71]:31), this incense-boat is a relatively standard Amiot design. However, another Amiot boat from the church of Saint-Anselme, Dorchester County, also made in 1837, is identical in shape but varies slightly in

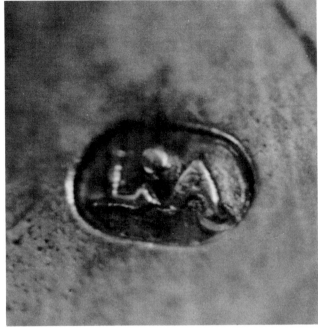

Fig. 17

ornament (IBC, Saint-Anselme [Dorchester] file, photos B-11 and B-12). The body of the Dorchester piece is enclosed in a plain fluted tongue pattern, and the splayed foot has a gadrooned rather than a plain border. The lid is similar except that an acanthus replaces the S-scrolls and a rose the small pairs of scrolls.

While Amiot repeated the basic design of these two boats throughout his career, the rose blossoms, acanthus leaves, S-scrolls, C-scrolls and the shells are all Neo-Rococo motifs possibly borrowed from contemporary English or American domestic silver. The overall design is also related to contemporary examples imported from France.

13 Tablespoon, ca. 1820–30

MEASUREMENTS
Length 21.7 cm. ($8\frac{9}{16}$ in.); weight 77 gm. (2 oz. 9 dwt.)

MARK
LA in oval (stamped twice on underside of handle) (fig. 18)

INSCRIPTION
Engraved on upper front of handle, IAH

PROVENANCE
H. Baron, Montreal; collection Francis W. Robinson, Grosse Pointe
Farms, Mi.; gift to DIA 23 July 1975.

Gift of Mr. and Mrs. Francis W. Robinson (75.35)

DESCRIPTION
Fiddle pattern spoon: shank of chamfered stem with two right-angled spurs
above bowl expanding to broad, shouldered upper section known as
"fiddleback"; end is rounded and turned down with lip and slight medial
ridge underneath; ovoid bowl with pointed end and small rounded drop at
back juncture of bowl and stem.

Fig. 18

A spoon was made from a single blank cut from a sheet of
silver of the desired thickness. The shape was roughed out
with the cross-peen of a hammer and smoothed with a
planishing hammer and files. The flat bowl was then shaped
by depressing it in a lead mold, or swage, with a complementary stamp struck by hammer (Diderot, "Orfèvre
grossier," pl. 11, figs. 5, 6, 13). Then the end of the handle
was bent and the spoon smoothed with a file and burnished.

The fiddle pattern was originally of French origin and
was popular in Quebec—without the spurs and with an oval
bowl—in the second and third quarters of the eighteenth
century. The pattern with spurs and ovoid bowl was adopted
in England at the end of the eighteenth century and then in
the United States, where it was most popular from 1810 to
1835. The English and American version of the fiddle pattern appeared in Quebec at about the same time as it did in
the United States. A distinctly French Canadian characteristic of the Amiot spoon, however, is the thick gauge of the
silver, in contrast to the relatively thin English and American flatware.

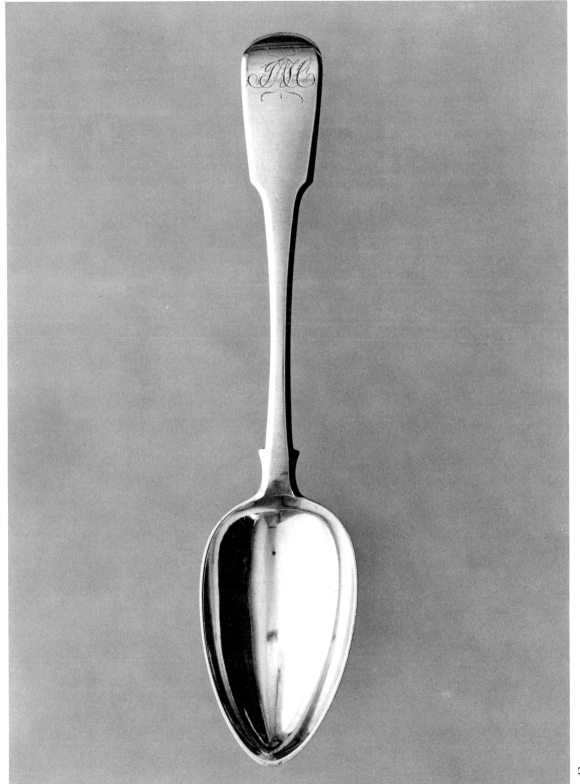

Jean-Baptiste Bequette

Quebec, Detroit, and Indiana

Active before 1817–ca. 1846

According to the register of Sainte Anne's Church, Detroit, Jean-Baptiste was born in the diocese of Quebec, son of Michel-Pierre Bequette (also Becquet or Bequet) and Geneviève Levasseur Borgia (BHC). Nothing is known of his early years, not even his date of birth. His parents were married at Quebec City on 18 May 1779, and two of their children were born in that city, Louise on 11 February 1780 and François on 27 April 1782. The family does not appear in records of Quebec or Montreal after this time (AQSG). His mother was related to the famous dynasty of Quebec sculptors the Levasseurs, and her second cousin, Marguerite Levasseur Borgia, was the wife of the silversmith Laurent Amiot. In view of the close familial ties of many of these silversmiths, Jean-Baptiste may have been apprenticed to Amiot.

Jean-Baptiste had lived in Detroit for seven years when he married Thérèse Durette (or Duret) on 27 July 1824, with Victor Rouquette, a Detroit silversmith, as a witness. Two children were born at Detroit, Thérèse-Marie-Justine on 2 October 1825, and Jean-Baptiste on 13 January 1827. Bequette was not present at the baptism of either child (BHC, RBMB, Sainte Anne, Detroit): about 1828 he moved his family to Indiana, where he made silver, probably Indian ornaments, from 1826 to about 1846 for William G. and

George W. Ewing, traders of Fort Wayne and Logansport, Indiana (FWR).

ATTRIBUTED TO JEAN-BAPTISTE BEQUETTE

14   Tablespoon, ca. 1810

MEASUREMENTS
Length 21.1 cm. ($8\frac{5}{16}$ in.); weight 47.9 gm. (1 oz. 11 dwt.)

MARK
Script JBB in rectangle (stamped twice on underside of handle)

INSCRIPTION
Engraved on upper front of handle, JC (Joseph Carrier)

PROVENANCE
Made for Joseph Carrier, Quebec City and Beaumont, Que. (FWR); collection Louis Carrier, Sainte-Anne de Bellevue, Que.; collection Lucille Carrier; gift to DIA 13 May 1964.

BIBLIOGRAPHY
DIA, *French in America*, p. 202, no. 548.

EXHIBITIONS
Detroit 1951b; Windsor 1953; Dearborn 1967

Gift of Robert H. Tannahill (acc. no. 64.85)

DESCRIPTION
Old English pattern: slender, lightly chamfered shank gradually expanding to rounded, turned-down end with lip and short medial ridge underneath; long ovoid bowl and rounded drop strengthening back juncture of bowl and stem.

Fig. 19

The design of this spoon is known as the Old English pattern, popular in England from the 1760s on and introduced into the United States and Canada about the 1780s. Relatively modest in weight and thickness, this spoon tends toward the lightness of English and American flatware. The maker's mark (fig. 19) was attributed to Jean-Baptiste Bequette by the late Louis Carrier, curator of the Château de Ramezay Museum, Montreal (FWR). It should be noted that Langdon (*Canadian Silversmiths,* p. 46; also *Marks,* p. 7) ascribes this mark to Jean-Baptiste Beguay (1786–1815+) of Quebec City, and he may prove to be the actual maker. No. 14 was undoubtedly made in Quebec; the style ended about 1815–1820.

No. 14

Louis-Philippe Boivin

Montreal

Active 1842–1857

Louis-Philippe Boivin was primarily a jeweler and watch-maker who is known to have worked in Montreal as early as 1842 (Traquair, p. 44). Very little is known about him: in the *Canada Directory* for 1851 he is listed as "Boivin, L. P., corner of Notre Dame and St. Vincent sts., importer of gold and silver watches, and jewellery—watches and clocks cleaned, repaired, and regulated" (p. 224). In the *Canada Directory* for 1857–58 (p. 320), he is mistakenly referred to as "E. P. Boivin." He was still an importer of clocks, watches, and jewelry, at the same location as in 1851, but now in partnership with Édouard E. Beaudry in the firm of Boivin & Beaudry. It has often been stated that Boivin was a dealer in silver but not a silversmith. How-ever, during this period jewelers often made silver flatware, and Boivin was probably no exception.

LOUIS-PHILIPPE BOIVIN

15 Dinner Fork, ca. 1845

MEASUREMENTS
Length 19.9 cm. (7¹³⁄₁₆ in.); weight 74.1 gm. (2 oz. 7 dwt.)

MARKS
LPB, lion passant, each in rectangle; sovereign's head in shaped cartouche (each stamped once on underside of handle) (fig. 20)

PROVENANCE
S. Breitman Antiques Ltd., Westmount (Montreal); collection Francis W. Robinson, Grosse Pointe Farms, Mi.; gift to DIA 23 July 1975.

Gift of Mr. and Mrs. Francis W. Robinson (75.38)

DESCRIPTION
Fiddle pattern: lightly chamfered shank of stem with two lower right-angled spurs gradually expanding to broad shouldered section with rounded, turned-up end and lip; four tines taper to pointed ends.

Four-tine silver dinner forks became popular in Quebec in the early eighteenth century, although in the United States they were not in general use until the succeeding century. Earlier American forks were small and had either two or three tines; they were used largely for dessert or sweet-meats, and such forks also made an occasional early appear-ance in Quebec. Eighteenth-century Quebec forks with four tines were usually in a provincial French fiddle pattern with upturned handle end and without spurs. They were often paired with tablespoons, and each table setting of dinner fork and tablespoon was known as a *couvert*. The dinner fork averaged between 7.5 inches (19 cm.) and 8 inches (20.3 cm.) in length; the tablespoon was about 8 inches or

Fig. 20

longer. These basic sizes continued into the mid-nineteenth century. The use of the silver dinner fork diminished by the end of the eighteenth century (cf. inventories in Appendix I), as English taste in domestic silver, in which the fork was not yet a popular eating implement, began to prevail in Quebec. The popular use of the four-tine dinner fork, however, was revived by the third decade of the nineteenth century, when it was being adopted on a wide scale in the United States. The dinner fork now followed the English and American version of the fiddle pattern (cf. No. 13), which, interestingly enough, recalls the basic shape of the eighteenth-century Quebec fork except for the addition of spurs.

55

Robert Cruickshank

Montreal

Active before 1774–1809

Robert Cruickshank was the foremost silversmith in Montreal in the second half of the eighteenth century and also one of that city's most prominent and wealthy citizens. He had an important hardware business as well as a large silver workshop and was one of the chief suppliers to the Northwest fur trade, the most important industry in Canada at that time. He furnished such important traders as McTavish, Frobisher & Co., James McGill, and the North West Company not only with prodigious quantities of Indian trade silver but also with items ranging from blankets to gunpowder. Eventually he himself became directly involved in the fur trade and was a shareholder in the North West Company. He was also active in the civic life of Montreal as a justice of the peace and a first warden of Christ Church, the Anglican cathedral (Carrier, p. 9).

Little is known of Cruickshank's background. He came from the British Isles and his name suggests that he was Scottish, yet the design and craftsmanship of his silver reflect an English training. He was in Montreal by 1774, when he signed a petition to the king from the English citizens of Montreal (Traquair, p. 15). He formed an early partnership with Michael Arnoldi, silversmith, but this was dissolved on 1 November 1784 (*GQ*, 14 October 1784). On 14 August 1789, Cruickshank, a widower with a daughter, married Ann Kay, a widow, at Christ Church. (Her first husband, William Kay, a Montreal merchant trading through Detroit and Mackinac, died on 25 July 1787.) She died on 10 December 1790 (ANQM, RBMB, Christ Church de Montréal).

As was the custom of the time, Cruickshank engaged numerous apprentices, including Michel Roy in 1791 (FWR, notes of Louis Carrier), Frederick Delisle in 1795, René Blache in 1796, Peter Bohle in 1800, and Narcisse Auclair in 1805 (Traquair, p. 16). Besides Indian trade silver, he produced quantities of domestic and ecclesiastical silver, the latter chiefly for Roman Catholic churches and convents. His silver was always of the highest quality, whether working with English or French designs. His reputation and commissions extended as far beyond the Montreal area as Detroit. In the fall of 1807 he voyaged to England and on his return passage died on board the *Everetta* on 16 April 1809 (*GQ*, 22 June 1809).

16 Ciborium, ca. 1750, by Guillaume Loir; dome of foot and cross replaced ca. 1790 by Robert Cruickshank

MEASUREMENTS
Height 24 cm. (9$\frac{7}{16}$ in.); diameter of bowl 11.3 cm. (4$\frac{7}{16}$ in.); diameter of base 12.1 cm. (4$\frac{3}{4}$ in.); weight 577.5 gm. (18 oz. 11 dwt.)

MARKS
Script RC in shaped outline (stamped once on cross finial and twice under foot); G crescent L under fleur-de-lis and two *grains de remède* (pellets), in shaped cartouche (stamped once inside basal rim; upper portion of mark, originally with a crown, is cut off at rim edge)

INSCRIPTION
Scratched under foot, HP-24-10

CONDITION
Small repair below knop

PROVENANCE
Reportedly church of Saint-Marcellin, Les Escoumins, Que.; S. Breitman Antiques Ltd., Westmount (Montreal); DIA purchase 16 October 1972.

BIBLIOGRAPHY
Fox, ''Liturgical Silver,'' pp. 101–2, fig. 5; Fox, *Traditional Arts*, no. 41 (ill.).

EXHIBITIONS
Windsor 1975

Elizabeth, Allan, and Warren Shelden Fund (acc. no. 72.467)

DESCRIPTION
Usual four separable sections: cover, bowl, stem, and foot. The interiors of both the bowl and the cover are electro-gilt (see Appendix II). The plain raised bowl has vertical sides, a rounded bottom, and an applied bead below the rim forming a bezel. The domed cover is raised in a plain compressed pear shape with a chased dentiled flange and a vertical seamed band, both applied to the rim. The finial, consisting of a flat cross and pedestal which are brazed together, is screwed to the center of the dome. A relatively short baluster stem, fashioned in the usual manner, has a spool with mid-molding, an inverted and stepped pyriform knop, a bell form, a dentiled collar knop, and a molded band. The knop has a stepped and gadrooned shoulder and an acanthus frieze below; the knop is raised and the ornament chased. The domed and splayed foot has four brazed parts: an upper raised dome, a dentiled flange similar to the cover, a *cyma reversa* molding, and an outer strengthening band.

Fig. 21. Robert Cruickshank, ciborium. H. 21.5 cm. National Gallery of Canada, Ottawa, acc. no. 16,864.

Guillaume Loir of Paris (active 1716–1769) was the maker of the original ciborium, but Robert Cruickshank partially refashioned it at a later date after it became damaged (such partial refashioning of old liturgical vessels was common in Quebec, as elsewhere). Cruickshank strictly adhered to Loir's original design, probably requested to do so by the priest or churchwardens who commissioned the repairs. As Cruickshank and Loir were both superior craftsmen and Cruickshank occasionally worked in a style similar to that of Loir, it is difficult to determine which part is the work of which silversmith. The situation is complicated further by the fact that Cruickshank is known to have used this particular design on at least one other occasion (fig. 21). Spectroscopic analysis does not provide an insight; the high silver readings of the knop and cover, and possibly the foot, at 99 percent, 98.81 percent, and 98.02 percent, suggest electroplating (see Appendix II). However, the bowl, with a reading of 95.5 percent, is within range of the Paris standard. A more certain clue to the attribution is provided by the presence of punch marks on certain sections (fig. 22). The mark of Guillaume Loir is stamped inside the basal rim. The very fact of its presence along with the mark of Cruickshank indicates, at the very least, that Cruickshank made this vessel from a pre-existing piece by Loir. Cruickshank's mark is also found on the foot, but under the upper dome. The placement of both makers' marks indicates that the outer molding and rim of the foot were by Loir and the domed part above the dentiled flange by Cruickshank. This attribution is supported by the fact that the quality of the silver patina of these two sections differs considerably: the silver quality of the entire upper portion of the ciborium is identical to that of the basal molding. Thus Cruickshank apparently replaced the upper foot, the cross finial (which also bears his mark), and possibly the bowl. As for the placement of Cruickshank's mark, when a British silversmith worked on an older piece he was required to affix his mark

Fig. 22

to any remade section; otherwise the piece was considered to be a forgery. Cruickshank, who had trained in Great Britain, was merely continuing this practice.

The design of this ciborium dates from about 1750, when Guillaume Loir made a similar piece for the church of Saint-Antoine de Tilly, Lotbinière County. The latter was acquired at the same time as a missal and an altar frontal at a cost of 400 livres (IBC, Saint-Antoine de Tilly file, photo C-12). Loir worked in a sober and restrained manner directly rooted in the late Louis XIV period. His work was characterized by a severity and a simplification of decorative elements, with a preference for classical motifs. He was concerned with the rhythmical horizontal alternation of broad smooth surfaces of metal with fine gadrooned or dentiled bands, or broad fluted or reeded bands. His vessels have highly polished surfaces and precise outlines. Loir's work was essentially in the late Louis XIV style, which, until mid-century at Paris, was still preferred for church plate over the more secular Louis XV style. The influence of the Louis XIV style was especially prominent in his work because most of it was ecclesiastical; in fact, he was one of the most important and productive makers of church plate in eighteenth-century Paris and included even Louis XV among his extensive clientele (Helft, p. 162). He was a member of a dynasty of Parisian silversmiths, including his uncle and former master Jean-Baptiste Loir (active 1689–1716), who were the semi-official suppliers to the market of New France. Guillaume made a "Royal Madonna and Child," 83.8 cm. high, for Louis XV in 1731–32, which the king presented to the Indian mission at Oka, Quebec, in 1749, where it still remains (Maurault, pp. 61, 62 [ill.]; Trudel, no. 40 [ill.]). Other works of his are found in Quebec collections.

Despite his Louis XIV orientation, however, Loir's work also foreshadows the later Louis XVI style. Such pieces as this ciborium were copied by later eighteenth-century Quebec silversmiths. Cruickshank was influenced by Loir, but his pieces are often more severe than those of the French master. Cruickshank limits his use of gadrooning and dentils, often eliminating them altogether, as on a ciborium he made for the church of Saint-Anne, Varennes, in 1802 at a cost of 447 livres (Morisset, *Varennes,* pl. 27; IBC, Varennes file, photo D-6). The stem has a plain inverted gourd-shape knop and a plain flange collar knop. The foot and cover have dentiled bands, but Cruickshank omits the gadrooning and acanthus frieze of Loir.

Thus, while Guillaume Loir created the design of the Detroit ciborium, the superb craftsmanship testifies to the skill of both silversmiths. This piece may have always belonged to the church of Saint-Marcellin, Les Escoumins. Originally known as Notre-Dame-de-Bon-Désir, it was a mission church from 1720 to 1862, when it was elevated to parish status and received its first resident priest (Magnan, p. 554).

ROBERT CRUICKSHANK

17 Chalice, foot ca. 1790 by Robert Cruickshank; stem and cup replaced after ca. 1875 by an anonymous maker

MEASUREMENTS
Height 27.5 cm. (10¹³⁄₁₆ in.); diameter of cup 9.5 cm. (3¾ in.); diameter of base 14.7 cm. (5¹³⁄₁₆ in.); weight 516.5 gm. (16 oz. 12 dwt.)

MARK
Script RC in shaped outline (stamped three times under foot)

INSCRIPTION
Engraved on basal molding, Hôpital Général, Sorel

PROVENANCE
Hôpital Général, Sorel, Que., until the late 1960s (letter of abbé Jacques Boisclair, chaplain); Jean Octeau, Montreal; DIA purchase 29 July 1969.

BIBLIOGRAPHY
BDIA 48 (1969):40 (ill.); Fox, "Liturgical Silver," p. 103, back cover (ill.).

Gift of Mrs. Allan Shelden in memory of Robert H. Tannahill (acc. no. 69.171)

DESCRIPTION
Usual sections, screwed together in conventional manner (see No. 2). The cup is raised in a slender bell shape with flared lip and gilt interior. The baluster stem has a small upper spool, an upper cushion torus knop, a spool with mid-molding, a raised urn-shaped knop, a small cylinder with molding, a bell form, and a lower cushion knop. The stem is devoid of ornament except for the stepped shoulders of the knops. The foot has an upper dome, a chased dentiled flange, *cyma reversa* molding, and a strengthening band; pricked crosses with foliage are on opposite sides of the upper dome. The chalice is fashioned in a manner similar to that of the ciboria and chalices discussed previously; however, one unusual constructional feature is an inserted cylindrical sleeve extending through the entire length of the stem proper, from the upper spool to the lower bell form (possibly a strengthening device).

The maker's mark on this piece (fig. 23) is extremely small and is more typical of those used by Cruickshank on small flatware and Indian trade silver. There is a brazing line below the lower torus, and the quality of the silver patina is noticeably different above and below this line, suggesting

Fig. 24. Laurent Amiot, chalice. H. 18.7 cm. National Gallery of Canada, Ottawa, acc. no. 16,861.

that the foot was fashioned at a different time from the rest of the chalice. Spectroscopic analysis shows an extreme spread in the silver percentage between the foot and other two sections, a difference of 4.55 percent, indicating that only the foot is original and that the cup and stem probably date from the late nineteenth century: the silver reading of the foot, 97.23 percent, is in keeping with the eighteenth-century standard, but the readings of 92.93 and 92.68 percent for stem and cup are more usual in later nineteenth-century church silver (the absence of gold and lead traces in the cup suggest an even later date—see Appendix II).

The style of stem and cup further supports a later attribution. While the overall design is ultimately inspired by the Neoclassic designs of Laurent Amiot (fig. 24), the especially elongated stem is more typical of the mid-nineteenth century as found in the oeuvre of François Sasseville (fig. 25). Numerous chalices of this type were copied by other Quebec silversmiths in the second half of the nineteenth century, and one almost identical with that at Detroit was made by Pierre Lespérance for the church of Saint-Louis, Lotbinière, in 1880 (Morisset, *Lotbiniére*, pl. 29). It is unlikely that Lespérance worked on the Detroit chalice, as he died in 1882. However, it could have been fashioned by a silversmith such as Ambroise Lafrance (1847–1905) of Quebec City, who served his apprenticeship under Sasseville and was a companion and successor to Lespérance.

While it is not possible to date the foot, it should be noted that a chalice of related design by Cruickshank is found in the Henry Birks Collection, Montreal (Langdon, *Canadian Silversmiths*, pl. 11). Cruickshank was an extremely skilled craftsman of British training, and although his domestic silver was largely in the English Neoclassic style, he succeeded in adapting himself to the Quebec taste for French designs in liturgical silver.

Fig. 25. François Sasseville, chalice, H. 24.3 cm. National Gallery of Canada, Ottawa, acc. no. 15, 836.1.

ROBERT CRUICKSHANK

18 Teapot, ca. 1802

MEASUREMENTS
Height 15.5 cm. (6⅛ in.); length 27.9 cm. (11 in.); length of oval 14 cm. (5½ in.); width of oval 10.7 cm. (4³⁄₁₆ in.); weight including handle 720.2 gm. (23 oz. 3 dwt.)

MARKS
Script RC in shaped outline (fig. 26); MONTREAL in rectangular cartouche (each stamped twice under bottom)

INSCRIPTION
Engraved on both sides, JCB (Jacques Bâby?)

CONDITION
Rectangular silver plate reinserted on one side and bright-cut decoration sketchily redone; small reinforcing plate applied under spout; spout rebrazed to pot; ring and wood handles later replacements

PROVENANCE
Reportedly made for Jacques (James) Bâby (1763–1833), Detroit, Sandwich, and Toronto; collection Dr. and Mrs. Clare S. Sandborn, Windsor, Ont.; collection Mr. and Mrs. William J. Marcoux, Jackson, Mi.; loan to DIA 21 February 1951.

BIBLIOGRAPHY
Fox, "French Canadian Silver," p. 79, fig. 5; Fox, *Traditional Arts,* no. 42 (ill.).

EXHIBITIONS
Windsor 1953; Windsor 1975

Lent by Mr. and Mrs. William J. Marcoux (Loan 5.51)

DESCRIPTION
Oval flat-bottomed pot with straight sides. The top has a flat perimeter, a gently concave shoulder, and a low domed lid with a riveted ring finger grip, a small vent hole, and an applied band forming a bezel. At the front of the pot, a cylindrical tapered spout, oval in section and applied over the strainer just above the basal molding, rises at an oblique angle. The body is seamed at the handle; the spout is seamed on the upper side. Balancing the spout is a looped wooden handle with a small thumb grip, inserted into two cylindrical sockets applied to the pot. The ends of the sockets are banded, and the bottom and top edges of pot each have an applied molding. Bright-cut and engraved ornament is repeated on both sides of the pot, including ribbon and a pendant cartouche enclosing the monogram JCB and foliate scrolls with two flower-and-leaf swags. At the top and the base of the pot are pricked linear patterns of dots and strokes.

This is one of about six known teapots by Robert Cruickshank. Silver teapots were rarely made in Quebec before 1800, as French Canadians were basically coffee drinkers. The few teapots used in the early eighteenth century were usually made of faience imported from Rouen and Marseilles. The advent of tea as a popular beverage came with the English regime, but those English newcomers who could afford silver preferred to import their tea services from England (Langdon, *Canadian Silversmiths,* p. 17). Toward the end of the eighteenth century Quebec silversmiths began to receive commissions for teapots. These reproduce the designs of imported English pieces and are usually in the Neoclassic style like this one.

As the Neoclassic style unfolded in England in the 1760s, a revolutionary new method for the making of silver holloware was developed, based on a new technological innovation, machine-rolled sheets of silver produced by rolling mills. Fully in the Neoclassic style, the Cruickshank teapot is made of this rolled sheet silver. Sheet silver production was introduced into the United States by the 1780s and must have been in use in Quebec by the end of the century, as this piece indicates. If there were no rolling mills in Quebec during this period, the rolled sheet silver must have been imported from England. The silversmith no longer had to melt coins and hammer his own sheets from the resultant cast silver ingots. Moreover, the rolled silver sheets were thinner and easier to handle. Now the silversmith simply drew a pattern on the sheet, cut out the components, bent them into the desired shapes, and then "seamed" or brazed them together.

In creating this teapot, Cruickshank cut an oval piece for the bottom, a long rectangular piece for the body, and appropriate shapes for the spout and sockets. These sections, except for the base, were then shaped on round stakes and seamed, by the handle, on the upper side of the spout, at the base, etc., until the assemblage of the body was com-

plete. The cover and shoulder were then shaped in the traditional manner in the hollow of a tree trunk and on the edge of a wood block. After these sections were added to the body, a wooden handle was slipped into the sockets of the pot and pins placed crosswise to keep it secure.

Although sheet silver permitted new efficiency, because of its thinness and relative fragility it could only be translated into a relatively limited range of shapes, including the cylinder, cone, and hemisphere, and decoration formed by embossing and chasing was no longer possible. For this reason the bright-cut technique became highly developed. Consisting of short shallow strokes at an angle, it compensated for the thinness of the silver while creating a very pleasing effect. Rolled silver sheets ushered in a dramatic alteration of the traditional craft methods of the silversmith and foreshadowed even greater mechanization yet to come, which would eventually destroy the craft. However, the design qualities of manufactured sheet silver coincided with the late eighteenth-century demands of the Neoclassic aesthetic: regularity and symmetry were emphasized, along with a rectilinear quality present in the shapes available with sheet silver. Decorative restraint was also important, as was lightness in appearance and construction.

These developments in technology and technique in effect determined Neoclassic designs, which, although they were complementary, were ultimately of English derivation. By 1800 domestic silver in Quebec, even by such makers as Laurent Amiot and Pierre Huguet dit Latour, imitated contemporary Neoclassic designs from England and the United States. Liturgical silver, however, still adhered to French prototypes.

While Cruickshank is the maker of this teapot, it is not certain that he executed the bright-cut ornament himself. The engraving is Neoclassic in spirit, fully in keeping with the design of the pot, and undoubtedly contemporary. Cruickshank may have given the task of engraving to a specialized silversmith-engraver; as in most large American cities, the trade for silver engraving in Quebec City and Montreal was handled by a few engraver-specialists. Little is known about the engravers working in Montreal during this period, and the engraver of this piece cannot yet be identified. The ornament here is quite charming but does not match the superb quality of similar ornament found, for example, on New York silver.

Cruickshank generally eschewed the use of engraved ornament even though its overall effect can be one of relatively Neoclassical restraint. Of course, he had to bow to a patron's wishes, but he preferred the pristine quality created by highly polished undecorated surfaces. When engraving was present, it was usually limited to the owner's initials. This aspect is seen in most other teapots by Cruickshank, especially one in the Henry Birks Collection, which is identical with the Marcoux teapot except for a knob finial and the absence of engraving (fig. 27).

The original owner of this piece is said to be the Honorable Jacques (James) Bâby of Detroit, Sandwich, and Toronto, as indicated by the "JCB" engraved on both sides of the pot; however, he did not have a middle initial "C," although he occasionally used his father's middle name of Duperon. (The only Bâby of this period with the initial "C" was Jacques' son, Thomas Charles (1806–1871), of Sandwich.) Jacques Bâby, son of Jacques Duperon Bâby and Susanne Reaume, was born at Detroit on 25 August 1763. He moved to Sandwich after 1796, where he was active as a merchant, landowner, and colonel of the militia for Kent County. He also had a very successful political career and in 1792 was appointed a member of the Executive and Legislative Councils of Upper Canada (Ontario) for life. From 1815 until his death on 19 Feburary 1833 he was inspector-general of Upper Canada, at which time he resided at York (Toronto). He was a member of that elite clique or plutocracy known as the "Family Compact"

Fig. 26

Fig. 27. Robert Cruickshank, teapot. H. 16.1 cm. Henry Birks Collection, Montreal, acc. no. C.210.

which controlled every facet of the political, economic, and social life of early Ontario. About 1802 Bâby married Elizabeth, daughter of James Abbott, judge and merchant of Detroit, and of Mary Barkle (also Baroness Von Brocklowe), formerly of Albany. The teapot was probably commissioned from Robert Cruickshank about this time (Casgrain, pp. 132–47). It was not an isolated commission, as Cruickshank supplied other domestic and even liturgical silver to the Detroit-Sandwich area, as well as large quantities of Indian trade silver.

19 Pair of Dessert Spoons, ca. 1790–1800

MEASUREMENTS
Length of right spoon 17.7 cm. (7 in.); weight of right spoon 31.9 gm. (1
oz. 1 dwt.); length of left spoon 17.9 cm. (7 in.); weight of left spoon 34.2
gm. (1 oz. 2 dwt.)

MARKS
Script RC in shaped outline; MONTREAL in rectangular cartouche (each
stamped once on underside of both handles) (fig. 28)

INSCRIPTION
Engraved on upper front of handles, W

PROVENANCE
From the Boston area; Ronald Bourgeault Antiques, Salem, Mass.; DIA
purchase 30 October 1974.

Elizabeth, Allan, and Warren Shelden Fund (acc. no. 74.120 a, b)

DESCRIPTION
Old English pattern: slender, lightly chamfered shank gradually expanding
to rounded, turned-down end with lip and short medial ridge underneath;
ovoid bowl and rounded drop strengthening back juncture of bowl and
stem.

Fig. 28

The lightness in weight and thin gauge of the silver, as well
as a certain delicacy in the execution, is typically English
rather than French Canadian. The dessert spoon followed
the designs of other spoons and was an intermediary size
between the teaspoon and tablespoon. Teaspoons averaged
about 5.5 inches (14 cm.) in length, dessert spoons about 7
inches (17.8 cm.), and tablespoons 8 inches (20.3 cm.) or
longer. The dessert spoon, like the teaspoon, was probably
of English derivation; the earliest known examples in
Quebec date from the late eighteenth century.

ROBERT CRUICKSHANK

20 Cross, ca. 1800

MEASUREMENTS
Length 25 cm. (9⅞ in.); width 18.7 cm. (7⅜ in.); weight 65.6 gm. (2 oz. 2 dwt.)

MARKS
Script RC in shaped outline; MONTREAL in rectangular cartouche (each stamped once at crossing on reverse side)

CONDITION
Severed lower arm reattached

PROVENANCE
Collection Henry Tucker, Mt. Clemens, Mi.; gift to DIA of his granddaughter 8 October 1952.

Gift of Miss Alice Tucker (acc. no. 52.212)

DESCRIPTION
Flat, thin cruciform pectoral ornament cut from sheet silver, each arm terminating in a series of semicircular receding bulges. The decorative treatment is limited to a few simple motifs engraved by means of short light strokes. A vine motif with leaves dominates the main section of the obverse side; on the reverse is an oval medallion at the crossing (which encloses the maker's mark; see fig. 29) and a repeated abstract floral design at the four ends. The top of the main arm is pierced with a small hole containing a ring so that the cross can be suspended from the neck.

Made for the Indian trade, the overall design is kept relatively simple. The most important requirement of this type of ornament was a highly polished surface; when ordering trade silver, fur traders usually specified that it be "thin and well-polished" (Barbeau, "Indian Trade Silver," p. 34). The thinness kept the silver relatively inexpensive, while the brilliant polish assured its appeal to Indian recipients, who valued these trinkets chiefly for their coruscating effect. Indians often covered themselves with silver crosses, pendants, and brooches, the silver serving both as an important medium of exchange and as a status symbol. Vast quantities were produced from 1775 to 1825 to satisfy the de-

Fig. 29

mands of the Indians and the fur trade. Cruickshank was one of the leading suppliers of silver for the Indian trade and first in quantity of production for Michigan and the surrounding area (*ibid.*, p. 29).

This cross represents a standard design for Indian trade silver. A similar cross by Cruickshank is at the Museum of the American Indian, Heye Foundation, New York (Langdon, "Canadian Silver," fig. 4). These relatively crude pieces could be produced easily, suggesting that they were not the product of the master but were made by apprentices or companions or were contracted out to lesser independent silversmiths, although the master's mark was affixed to the finished article. They were then sold in bulk to fur traders such as the North West Company, who exchanged them with the Indians for furs. This cross was found among the personal effects of Henry Tucker of Mt. Clemens upon his death in 1855. Tucker was active as a fur trader in the Upper Great Lakes and probably acquired it from Indians of that region (FWR).

70

ROBERT CRUICKSHANK

21 Cross of Lorraine, ca. 1800

MEASUREMENTS
Length 10.5 cm. (4⅛ in.); width of upper arm 4.4 cm. (1¾ in.); width of lower arm 4.9 cm. (1¹⁵⁄₁₆ in.); weight 12.5 gm. (8 dwt.)

MARK
Script RC in shaped outline (stamped once at upper crossing on reverse) (fig. 30)

PROVENANCE
Found in Indian burial ground, Albion, Mi., 1844; collection Marygrove College; gift to DIA 8 October 1952.

Gift of Marygrove College (acc. no. 52.223)

DESCRIPTION
Thin flat cross with two transverse bars, cut from sheet silver. The main shaft tapers slightly from the base, with a large almost semi-circular bulge and a smaller bulge above, up to a pierced trilobate terminal with a metal ring. The transverse bars are plain and flat-edged with a double lobe at the ends. The surface is treated with a lightly engraved zigzag pattern or rouletting, which outlines the edge. Clusters of five punch marks are repeated at roughly equal intervals on the shaft and bars.

Fig. 30

Another example of Indian trade silver, this type of small pectoral cross is known as a Cross of Lorraine because of its double transverse bar.

Michel Forton

Quebec City, Mackinac, and Detroit
1754–ca. 1816

Michel Forton was born in Quebec City in 1754 and apprenticed to Joseph Schindler (Carrier, p. 8). He accompanied Schindler to Mackinac (Michilimackinac) in the spring of 1775. On 11 June 1776 he was in Detroit, where he was a witness to the marriage of Antoine Bernard and Catherine Dubreuil (BHC, RBMB, Sainte Anne, Detroit). The following year he was again in Detroit, where, on 8 August, he testified on behalf of Schindler, who was on trial for making silver below standard (see p. 142). In the court proceedings, Forton is referred to as "apprentice to the aforesaid prisoner" (*Remembrancer,* pp. 188–91). After the Detroit adventure, Forton returned to either Montreal or Quebec City and eventually settled at the latter. On 10 July 1794, at Quebec City, he signed a declaration of loyalty to the Constitution and Government (*GQ*). On 22 October of the following year he signed a petition drawn up by silversmiths requesting exemption from a new ordinance prohibiting the use of a forge in Quebec City or its suburbs "which is not either wholly walled with, or wholly inclosed with brick or stone, or lathed and well plastered." The other petitioners were François Ranvoyzé, James Hanna, Laurent Amiot,

James Orkney, Jean Amiot, and François Picard (ANQQ).

From 1795 on, Forton is variously described as a merchant silversmith or jeweler, or both. He was a silversmith and dealer and possibly an importer as well, as can be inferred from the following notice in *La Gazette de Québec* of 9 August 1810: "Tuesday four men entered the shop of Mr. Forton, silversmith, on rue [Côte de] la Montagne, where they remained for some time without buying anything, and when they had left, he discovered four teaspoons and a tablespoon were missing. Fortunately, the spoons were silvered [plated]." (These spoons were undoubtedly imported, as the technique of silverplating had not yet been introduced into Quebec.) There are also numerous references to Forton as a landlord, and he was considerably involved in real estate. On 18 February 1813, James Tod[d?], a merchant, leased from him for three years, at 50 louis per year, the third story of a house at the corner of rues Saint-Georges and Laval (ANQQ, Louis-T. Besserer minutes). One of the last references to Forton is as subscriber to the Quebec Fire Society on 19 October 1815 (*GQ*). He died shortly thereafter.

Fig. 31

MICHEL FORTON

22 Mustard Spoon, ca. 1790

MEASUREMENTS
Length 11.3 cm. ($4\frac{7}{16}$ in.); weight 9.8 gm. (6 dwt.)

MARK
MF in rectangle (stamped once on underside of handle) (fig. 31)

INSCRIPTION
Engraved on upper front of handle, Cann(?) crest (Fairbairn, p. 95, pl. 34, 14)

PROVENANCE
Collection Louis Carrier, Sainte-Anne de Bellevue, Que.; collection Francis W. Robinson, Grosse Pointe Farms, Mi.; gift to DIA 23 July 1975.

BIBLIOGRAPHY
DIA, *French Canada,* p. 39, no. 152.

EXHIBITIONS
Detroit 1946; Detroit 1951a

Gift of Mr. and Mrs. Francis W. Robinson (75.37)

DESCRIPTION
Old English pattern: long, slender handle gradually expanding to rounded, turned-down end with slight lip underneath; deep, almost hemispherical bowl and rounded drop at back juncture of bowl and stem.

Mustard spoons of the late eighteenth and early nineteenth centuries were usually in the shape of miniature ladles, as in this example (cf. No. 47).

75

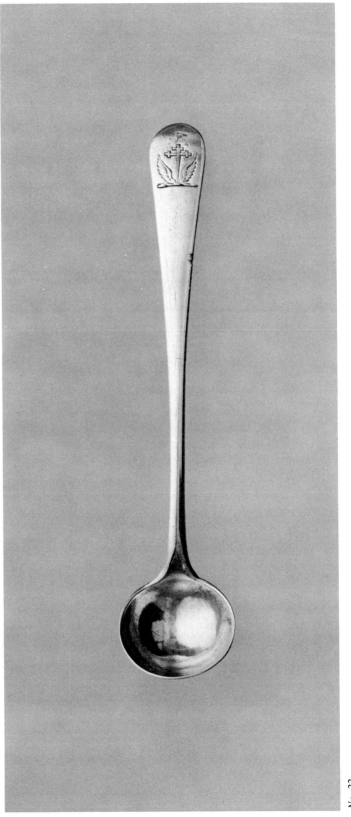

Pierre Foureur dit Champagne

Montreal

1756–1795+

Pierre, son of Louis Foureur dit Champagne, a sculptor, and of Catherine Guertin, was born in Montreal in 1756 (Morisset, "L'instrument," p. 148). He was a witness to the marriage of François Larsonneur, silversmith, and Marguerite Petel at Notre-Dame Church, Montreal, on 30 June 1783 and was godfather to their son, François-Stanislas, baptized at the same church on 18 January 1785 (ANQM). Pierre's sister, Charlotte, married Dominique Rousseau, a silversmith active in Montreal and Detroit. On 21 December 1795, Pierre was a signatory to the will of the Montreal sculptor Philippe Liébert, and there refers to himself as a "merchant-silversmith" (ANQM, Jean-Baptiste Desève minutes). He was a gilder as well as a silversmith (Morisset, "L'instrument," p. 148). Few of his silver pieces survive, but among them are a pax at the Mistassini Indian Mission, Quebec, and Indian trade silver at the McCord Museum, Montreal.

ATTRIBUTED TO PIERRE FOUREUR DIT CHAMPAGNE

23 Pair of Tablespoons, ca. 1802

MEASUREMENTS
Length of right spoon 20.3 cm. (8 in.); weight 52 gm. (1 oz. 14 dwt.); length of left spoon 20.2 cm. (8 in.); weight of left spoon 46.2 gm. (1 oz. 10 dwt.)

MARKS
PC in rectangle (stamped once on underside of each handle) (fig. 32)

Fig. 32

INSCRIPTION
Engraved on upper front of handles, JBB (Jean-Baptiste Beaugrand)

CONDITION
Ends of bowls worn

PROVENANCE
Made for Jean-Baptiste Beaugrand, Detroit and Fremont, Ohio: collections Sophie Beaugrand Rawson, Joseph Rawson, Sophia Elizabeth Rawson Harris, Jane Harris Crane; loan to DIA 17 January 1956.

Lent by Verner W. Crane

DESCRIPTION
Old English pattern: slender, relatively flat shank gradually expanding to rounded, almost pointed, turned-down end with lip; ovoid bowl and rounded, slightly beveled drop strengthening back juncture of bowl and stem.

The original attribution of these spoons to Pierre Foureur dit Champagne was made by Louis Carrier. According to family tradition, silver buckles and other silver items were sent to Montreal, where they were fashioned into a set of spoons for Jean-Baptiste Beaugrand. These two spoons are part of that set; a third spoon also survives and belongs to another Beaugrand descendant in Ohio.

Jean-Baptiste Beaugrand, Indian trader and merchant, was born in Trois-Rivières, Quebec, in 1768. He was the son of Jean-Baptiste Beaugrand, who emigrated to Canada from Bordeaux, France, and of Marie-Anne Alain. Sometime before 1796 Beaugrand settled in Detroit, where he married Marguerite Chabert on 29 July 1802 (BHC, MSS index). The following year he was appointed lieutenant for the First Regiment of the Wayne County Militia and in 1805 was made captain for the Second Regiment. In 1807 he had a trading post on the Raisin River, where he temporarily moved his family, but he soon sent them back to Detroit. By 1811 he had a post on the Maumee River; it was destroyed by the Wyandots during the War of 1812. In 1822 he was in Lower Sandusky (now Fremont), Ohio, and brought his family there from Detroit in 1823. He died there in February 1826 (FWR).

Robert Hendery

Montreal

Active 1837–1897

Robert Hendery, originally from Scotland, came to Montreal before 1837. He had his own business after 1840 and by 1850 was in partnership with Peter Bohle (1786–1862), also a silversmith. Bohle and Hendery were silver manufacturers, or makers to the trade, and were the suppliers of the firms of George Savage & Son and, after 1850, of Savage & Lyman. In 1855 Bohle and Hendery had an exhibit at the Paris International Exhibition (Traquair, p. 21). Their partnership was later dissolved, probably in 1856. Hendery continued to work for Savage & Lyman, and in the *Canada Directory* for 1857–58 (p. 360) he is listed as a working silversmith and plater, at 154 Craig Street. In an advertisement in *Mackay's Montreal Directory* for 1863–64 (p. 433), he is described as a silversmith, spoonmaker, and plater, at 112 Craig Street.

In 1864 Hendery engaged as an apprentice John Leslie, newly arrived in Montreal from Aberdeen, Scotland. By 1887 Leslie was taken into partnership with Hendery, and the firm's name was changed from Robert Hendery and Co. to Hendery & Leslie. These firms were the most important Canadian silver manufacturers in the late nineteenth century, supplying dealers across Canada. Robert Hendery retired in 1895 and died in 1897. The firm of Hendery & Leslie was bought out by Henry Birks & Sons in 1899. The identity or quality marks on silver produced by the Hendery firms were a lion rampant in an oval and a sovereign's head in a square with clipped corners. The individual dealer usually added his own mark (Langdon, *Canadian Silversmiths,* pp. 23–24, 83–84).

ROBERT HENDERY

24 Reliquary Cross, ca. 1860

MEASUREMENTS
Length 9.5 cm. (3¾ in.); length of arm 4 cm. (1 9/16 in.); depth 0.8 cm. (5/16 in.); weight 34.2 gm. (1 oz. 2 dwt.)

MARKS
Lion rampant in oval; sovereign's head in square with clipped corners (each stamped once under lid) (fig. 33)

INSCRIPTIONS
Engraved on front, Jesus Hostie ("host"); engraved on back, Sang Precieux ("precious blood") and Marie Immaculee ("Immaculate Heart of Mary")

PROVENANCE
Convent of the Adoratrices du Précieux-Sang, Montreal; H. Baron, Montreal; DIA purchase 30 October 1957.

BIBLIOGRAPHY
DIA, *Tannahill*, p. 68.

Gift of Robert H. Tannahill (acc. no. 57.141)

DESCRIPTION
Cruciform pectoral reliquary case, rectangular in section with flat back-plate and applied sides. A flat lid, hinged at the upper end, fits over the case and has an applied horizontal end-plate with a perforated center which overlaps the lower end of case, also perforated. A pendant teardrop, with a small threaded rod, screws through both perforations, securing the lid. The upper end of the case has a cast and applied baluster finial with a ring containing a larger ring for suspending the case from the neck. The upper end of the lid has an applied shield with five grooved horizontal bands, known as a barry of five. A fine pricked zigzag band outlines the front and back edges of the case. A heart with a wound and an upper cross are engraved at the crossing of the front; on the back, a heart is transpierced by a dagger.

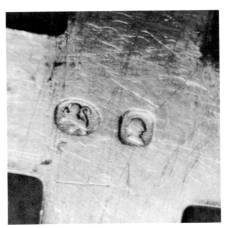

Fig. 33

This reliquary case, actually a nun's professional cross, was worn by a nun of the Convent of the Adoratrices du Précieux-Sang. The heart with wound and cross on the front of the case represents the Sacred Heart of Jesus, a popular Roman Catholic cultic devotion. The phrase "Jesus Hostie" accompanying this heart refers to the Eucharistic Host. The heart transpierced by a dagger on the back symbolizes the Immaculate Heart of Mary, as indicated by the words "Marie Immaculee." On the transverse bar "Sang Precieux" refers to the "Precious Blood" of Jesus Christ. It was to this cult that the order of nuns of the same name was especially dedicated.

No. 24b

Huguet dit Latour

Montreal

There are three silversmiths with the surname Huguet dit Latour: Pierre, his brother Louis, and Pierre II, son of Pierre. All were active in the same workshop and used the mark PH in a square, sometimes accompanied by the word "Montreal" in a rectangle.

PIERRE HUGUET DIT LATOUR. 1749–1817

Pierre Huguet I was born in Quebec City on 24 January 1749, the son of Claude Huguet dit Latour, a tailor, and his second wife, Marie-Charlotte Lamothe (Tanguay, 4:545). He began his career as a wig-maker and, when he moved to Montreal early in 1769, expanded his trade to include perfumes and jewelry. He was producing Indian trade silver by 1778 in his workshop at his residence on Notre-Dame sud near rue Saint-Sulpice, in Montreal (Morisset, "Un perruquier-orfèvre," p. 28). His new undertaking prospered, and soon he was letting large contracts for Indian ornaments. On 15 September 1781, he engaged François Larsonneur, a silversmith, to make eight hundred ear bobs monthly for a year (Massicotte, pp. 284–85). By 1800 he had become one of the major suppliers of Indian trade silver to the Northwest fur trade, rivaling Robert Cruickshank. Over the next two decades his workshop became noted for its ecclesiastical plate and was the chief supplier to the Montreal area. His church commissions prior to 1800 had been minimal, although he produced some silver for the church of Notre-Dame in Montreal, as indicated in the account books of the parish vestry. Pierre's active period terminated in 1812, when he transferred the business to his son Pierre II.

Pierre was frequently referred to as a merchant-silversmith and was probably more of a silver manufacturer, the actual silver being made in a large workshop under the direction of his brother Louis before 1792, and sometime thereafter under that of his son. It was Louis who probably taught the craft to both Pierres. Among the elder Pierre's apprentices were Michel Letourneau, who was engaged for four years on 21 August 1785; Augustin Lagrave, engaged for seven years on 10 October 1791 (the agreement was cancelled in 1797); Faustin Gignon, engaged for seven years on 30 March 1795; François Blache, engaged for five years on 25 September 1797; Salomon Marion, engaged for five years on 23 July 1798; and Paul (Hippolyte) Morand, engaged for three years on 28 April 1802 (ibid., p. 287).

Pierre was quite wealthy when he died, having speculated successfully in real estate and other business ventures. He married three times: Charlotte Desève, widow of Jean Leheup, 26 February 1770; Josephte Valois, 16 November 1788; and Marie-Louise Dalciat, widow of Claude Petitclair, watchmaker, 24 October 1809 (ANQM, RBMB, Notre-Dame de Montréal).

Louis-Alexandre was born on 10 August 1754 in Quebec City (Tanguay, 4:545) and was apprenticed there to Joseph Schindler on 22 December 1766 (ANQQ, Claude Louet minutes). He was living in Montreal by 22 January 1776, when he married Madeleine You dit Rochefort at Notre-Dame Church (ANQM). It was probably about this time that he began working for his brother Pierre, and he directed Pierre's workshop until his dismissal sometime before 1792. On 24 July of that year he contracted with Jacques Laselle, a trader of Detroit and Montreal, to go to Detroit, where he would "work in silver" (ANQM, Louis Chaboillez minutes). He died before 1795, as his wife was remarried to Charles Duval, silversmith, at Notre-Dame Church, Montreal, on 6 September 1795 (ANQM).

Pierre was born in Montreal in 1771 to Pierre I and his first wife, Charlotte Desève. Having served his apprenticeship under his uncle Louis, he directed his father's workshop from about 1792 on and carried on the entire enterprise from 1812 until his death in 1829. He never married, and bequeathed his estate to his half-sister Agathe-Henriette, widow of a Captain McDonnell (Massicotte, p. 287).

Because all three Huguets used the same mark, each piece must be studied to establish the maker. Style alone is frequently unreliable because many designs were repeated. The problem is further compounded by the presence in the Huguet workshop of numerous active apprentices and companions who undoubtedly used their master's mark, but their activity was probably limited largely to Indian ornaments and smaller wares. Louis was responsible for much of the production before 1792, largely Indian trade silver.

Pierre and his son are credited with the subsequent production, which included much ecclesiastical and domestic plate. Pieces after 1812 are likely by Pierre II.

PIERRE HUGUET DIT LATOUR

25 Ciborium, ca. 1805

MEASUREMENTS
Height 27.6 cm. (10⅞ in.); diameter of bowl 12.8 cm. (5¹⁄₁₆ in.); diameter of base 14.4 cm. (5¹¹⁄₁₆ in.); weight 702.5 gm. (22 oz. 11 dwt.)

MARK
PH in rectangle (stamped five times under foot) (fig. 34)

CONDITION
Threaded connectors relined

PROVENANCE
Reportedly church of Saint-Martin (Ile Jésus), near Montreal; Jean Octeau, Montreal; DIA purchase 5 November 1969.

BIBLIOGRAPHY
BDIA 48 (1969):37 (ill.).

Robert H. Tannahill Fund (acc. no. 69.263)

DESCRIPTION
Four separate sections, cover, bowl, stem, and foot, all fashioned largely by hammering and assembled in customary manner. The cover is raised in a low central dome and curved outer shoulder with an everted rim, and has an applied outer flange and vertical band. A flat cross finial on a small cast orb is brazed to the cover. The interiors of the cover and bowl are mercury-gilt. The bowl is plain, with vertical, slightly tapering sides and a bottom with a rounded edge and low convex center. A bead, forming a bezel, is applied below the rim, and a disc with a threaded rod under the bottom.

The baluster stem proper consists of an upper cylinder (with an inserted threaded sleeve), a dentiled collar knop, a spool with mid-molding, a disc, knop, molded band, and lower flared and molded cylinder which contains a projecting threaded rod. The central knop, raised in an archaic inverted pyriform with prominent shoulder, has chased upper and lower friezes of alternating long and short gadroons, with matte borders and a small bellflower at the end of each short gadroon. The second lower collar knop, containing a threaded sleeve, is brazed to the cylindrical projection of the foot. Each collar knop is a disc with a chased and applied dentiled band. The domed and splayed foot has a chased dentiled flange and a plain *cyma reversa* (or reverse ogee) outer molding with a strengthening band.

The slight convexity of the bottom of the bowl facilitated cleansing of the ciborium as well as making it easier to remove the small hosts. The overall design of this ciborium

Fig. 34

is of late Louis XIV inspiration and is most immediately associated with the work of Guillaume Loir of Paris (see No. 16). Such features as the dentiled bands alternating with broad plain surfaces, the form of the knop with its gadrooning, and the *cyma reversa* molding of the foot are found in Loir's work. Huguet's piece, however, lacks the subtlety of design evident in the work of the Parisian master. The various elements are not as harmoniously integrated; the bowl is too large, the foot a little too low. The design is not only retardataire but also somewhat provincial in treatment, although technically competent.

Huguet repeated this design on numerous occasions, a noteworthy example being at the church of Saint-Joachim, Pointe-Claire, in the vicinity of Saint-Martin (IBC, Pierre Huguet file, photo A-5). The two ciboria are almost identical in every aspect, including dimensions. The only real difference is that the Pointe-Claire ciborium has been marked four times and the Detroit piece five. According to Gérard Morisset, all the silver at Saint-Martin except a sanctuary lamp was acquired after 1802. Only the lamp (by Robert Cruickshank), which dates from 1800, is mentioned in the parish account books (Morisset, "Saint-Martin," pp. 604–5). Huguet also made a censer, an incense-boat, and a holy water stoup for this church. The stoup is now at Detroit (No. 26).

26 Holy Water Stoup and Aspergill, ca. 1805–10

MEASUREMENTS
Stoup (69.261): height including handle 28.1 cm. (11$\frac{1}{16}$ in.); height 18.6 cm. (7$\frac{5}{16}$ in.); diameter of shoulder 19.3 cm. (7$\frac{5}{8}$ in.); diameter of base 11.3 cm. (4$\frac{7}{16}$ in.); weight 693.4 gm. (22 oz. 6 dwt.). *Aspergill* (sprinkler): length 24.7 cm. (9$\frac{3}{4}$ in.); weight 130.4 gm. (4 oz. 4 dwt.)

MARKS
PH (one P is slightly effaced) in rectangle (stamped twice under foot); NTREA (for Montreal) in rectangular cartouche (stamped once under foot)

CONDITION
Poorly brazed repair on shoulder by collar; dents on shoulder (about 1 in. long) and on lip, as well as smaller dents scattered over surface. Aspergill repaired at head and upper handle; head dented

PROVENANCE
Church of Saint-Martin (Ile Jésus); Jean Octeau, Montreal; DIA purchase 5 November 1969.

BIBLIOGRAPHY
IBC, Saint-Martin (Ile Jésus) file, photo C-5 (photographed by Gérard Morisset 26 September 1942); Morisset, "Saint-Martin," pp. 602 (ill.), 605; *BDIA* 48 (1969):38 (ill.); Fox, "French Canadian Silver," pp. 79, 80, fig. 6; Fox, *Traditional Arts,* no. 43.

EXHIBITION
Windsor 1975

Josephine and Ernest Kanzler Fund (acc. nos. 69.261, 69.262)

DESCRIPTION
Raised "dropped bottom" bucket: above the swelling shoulder, is an applied cavetto collar and a vertical rim with an intervening large bead, wrought as a unit and seamed (vertical seam under handle). The swelling shoulder is bright-cut engraved with two patterns of interlaced garlands, the smaller one showing a leaf laurel with two berries, the larger a three-leafed laurel with two berries. The lower bucket is chased with a double-outlined tongue frieze, each tongue linked by an upper linear festoon. The circular domed foot is splayed and stepped with a chased gadrooned border and outer rim. The foot is raised and the border is swaged as a unit, except for the drawn and applied rim band.

The cylindrical arched handle, with a ball knop at its apex, tapers to a molding near each end. The handle is composed of seven brazed elements: the knop, two curving arms, molded bands, and L-shaped cylindrical ends. Each arm is shaped in two halves and seamed at top and bottom, as was the knop, which has a vertical seam around its circumference. The handle ends are inserted into sockets of two cast and chased angel-head brackets, attached at opposite sides of the mouth by four small rivets. Accompanying the stoup is an aspergill with a plain cylindrical shaft and a compressed, spherical, perforated head.

Fig. 35

No. 26

The holy water stoup (or aspersorium) is a receptacle for the holy water used in the Asperges, or ritual sprinkling, of the Mass or other liturgical rites. Originally a liner, possibly of tin, was inserted into the mouth of the bucket. This stoup is one of the best known by Pierre Huguet. Although dependent on numerous sources, especially the work of Laurent Amiot, the design of this piece is a very personal creation, and Huguet repeated it in almost all of his stoups.

The basic form of the bucket, with a ''dropped bottom,'' is reminiscent of Ranvoyzé's later stoups (*Ranvoyzé,* no. 10 [ill.]) and contrasts with the more classical urn shape used by Amiot (Langdon, *Canadian Silversmiths,* pl. 10). Nevertheless, this form appears to be a uniquely Canadian reinterpretation of the Louis XVI form of Amiot, but it has been so transformed that it defies precise stylistic classification. It is best referred to as being in a classical mode. The decorative motifs are more obviously related to the Louis XVI style, and the garlands on the shoulder of the bucket were borrowed from the decorative repertoire of Amiot (Morisset, *Cap-Santé,* pl. 16), but Huguet adds a personal note, as they are now bright-cut rather than embossed in low relief (cf. No. 8). This technique creates a shimmering or faceted effect, especially when contrasted with a highly burnished surface, as in this stoup. Huguet was one of the few Quebec silversmiths to use bright-cut engraving on church silver, and this application was confined largely to the Montreal area. The technique was borrowed from English Neoclassic domestic silver of the late eighteenth century. It is not certain whether Huguet executed this engraving himself or subcontracted it to a silversmith-engraver: he used this type of decoration with such frequency that he may have mastered the engraving technique himself. The tongue motif of the lower bucket was also derived from Amiot, and Huguet again treats this borrowing in a unique manner, as the usual fluting is now absent. A final decorative element, the gadrooning of the foot, is most frequently found in Louis XIV designs. Overall, Huguet succeeds in creating a personal design of classical inspiration. He reshapes a standard Louis XVI form and combines it with Louis XIV and Louis XVI motifs, the latter executed by means of an English Neoclassic technique.

The design of this piece recalls two other stoups by Huguet, both fashioned in 1808. One is at the church of Sainte-Anne, Varennes (Morisset, *Varennes,* pl. 29), the other at the Musée Notre-Dame in Montreal (Traquair, pl. 14a). Although the Notre-Dame stoup is similar in form, technique, and decoration, it is larger and the decoration has been slightly elaborated.

The NTREA mark (fig. 35) is a partial impression from the same punch that was used for MONTREAL (fig. 37) on No. 28.

27 Incense-boat, ca. 1820

MEASUREMENTS
Height 10.4 cm. ($4\frac{1}{16}$ in.); length of boat 17.9 cm. ($7\frac{1}{16}$ in.); length of base 8.5 cm. ($3\frac{3}{8}$ in.); weight 265 gm. (8 oz. 10 dwt.)

MARK
PH in rectangle (stamped twice under foot)

CONDITION
Joining of foot and boat and vertical rim of foot repaired; spoon and chain attachment lost

PROVENANCE
S. Breitman Antiques Ltd., Westmount (Montreal); DIA purchase 6 March 1974.

Elizabeth, Allan, and Warren Shelden Fund (acc. no. 74.4)

DESCRIPTION
The raised oval foot is molded and splayed, with an embossed and chased border of interlaced alternating bead and ellipse and applied high vertical rim. The front of the raised, shell-like boat is drawn to a long curved pouring spout with a rounded and turned-down end; the back crests in a rounded end. The boat is encircled by a frieze of fluted tongues with a chased groove and dot on their intervening matte ridges. The scallops of the tongues are tangent to a shaped, molded, and banded rim with a bead applied to the edge. A small ring is brazed to the rim on the left side, directly below the hinge. Originally a small spoon and chain were attached to the ring; this was used to transfer the grains of incense from the boat to the censer.

The cover is in two sections, a fixed, upcurved back-plate and a front lid with a four-part pinned hinge. The hinge plates are brazed underneath the cover. A bead molding is applied to the edge of both sections, and the ornament is embossed and chased. On the back-plate, in an arched reserve with molded edge, is a fluted anthemion with two S-scrolls on a matte ground. This motif, in a similar but elongated reserve, is repeated on the hinged front with an upper scrolled palmette.

The attribution of this incense-boat to Huguet is made with a number of reservations. The design is unlike the shallow, elliptical incense-boats usually produced by the Huguet workshop (Langdon, *Canadian Silversmiths,* pl. 18b); however, a similar design was used on occasion by two of Huguet's contemporaries, Laurent Amiot (see No. 12), and

Salomon Marion (1782–1830), who served his apprenticeship under Pierre Huguet I (*Canadian Art* 13 [1956]:295 [ill.]), and thus it could have been adopted by one of the Huguets. This design was directly inspired by numerous similar pieces which were imported from France in the early nineteenth century.

The elemental composition of this piece is unusual, as there is a rather low gold count. Such a count is possible in French silver of the late 1820s and after, but its occurrence in Quebec silver of the early nineteenth century is a definite oddity (see the discussion in Appendix II).

The maker's mark on this piece (fig. 36) was not made from the same punch as that on the other Huguet pieces in this catalogue (see figs. 34–35, 37). The most obvious differences are the absence of the rounded corners of the rectangular frame, the greater thickness of the letters, and the smaller serifs, which do not extend to the left, as in the usual Huguet mark. This mark may be from another Huguet punch or may be spurious and modern.

Thus at present the attribution ot this incense-boat to Huguet remains uncertain. It may prove to be a French piece of the 1830s or slightly later. If it was in fact made by a member of the Huguet family, the style suggests that it was fashioned by Pierre Huguet dit Latour II.

Fig. 36

28 Pair of Tablespoons, ca. 1790–1800

MEASUREMENTS
Length of right spoon 22 çm. (8$\frac{11}{16}$ in.); weight of right spoon 82.1 gm. (2 oz. 13 dwt.); length of left spoon 22.2 cm. (8$\frac{3}{4}$ in.); weight of left spoon 84.7 gm. (2 oz. 14 dwt.)

MARKS
PH in rectangle (stamped twice on underside of both handles); MONTREAL in rectangle (stamped once on underside of both handles)

INSCRIPTION
Engraved on upper front of handles, JC (Jacques Cartier)

PROVENANCE
Reportedly made for Jacques Cartier (1750–1813), Saint-Antoine-sur-Richelieu, Que.; Jean Octeau, Montreal; DIA purchase 29 July 1969.

Elizabeth, Allan, and Warren Shelden Fund (acc. nos. 69.173, 69.174)

DESCRIPTION
Old English pattern: slender, lightly chamfered shank gradually expanding to rounded, turned-down end with lip and short medial ridge underneath; ovoid bowl and rounded drop strengthening back juncture of bowl and stem.

Fig. 37

These are two of a set of six spoons; the others are in private collections in the Detroit area. The ''PH'' mark (fig. 37) is an early impression from the same punch that was used for the marks on Nos. 25 and 26 (figs. 34 and 35), the latter being the latest. As the puncheon becomes worn, the letters become thicker, and the spaces between the letters and the outer frame are reduced, disappearing entirely in spots.

The use of swages in making spoons resulted in some standardization in those produced by an individual silversmith. Another spoon identical with these two but belonging to another set and having the engraved initials MR is in the collection of Francis W. Robinson. These spoons are said to have been made for Jacques Cartier, a wealthy grain merchant of Saint-Antoine-sur-Richelieu, member of the House of Assembly of Lower Canada (Quebec) for Surrey (later Verchères) from 1804 to 1809, and colonel of the militia for the Richelieu district. His grandson was the illustrious Sir George-Étienne Cartier, who was prime minister of United Canada (comprising the provinces of Ontario and Quebec) from August 1858 to May 1862, and who subsequently, with Sir John A. Macdonald, was one of the founding fathers of the Dominion of Canada.

Augustin Lagrave

Montreal, Detroit, and Sandwich

1777–1825

Born at Montreal in 18 September 1777, Augustin was the son of Antoine Lagrave, a carter, and Thérèse Duperon (ANQM, RBMB, Notre-Dame de Montréal). On 10 October 1791 he was apprenticed to Pierre Huguet dit Latour (Massicotte, p. 287); his indenture was cancelled on 6 March 1797 (ANQM, Jean-Baptiste Desève minutes). Lagrave remained in Montreal for the next several years and in 1799 signed the address to General Robert Prescott, governor-in-chief of Canada, at his departure from Quebec for England (*GQ*, 25 July 1799). On 26 September 1800, Lagrave contracted with Jacques and François Laselle to go to Detroit, probably to work as a silversmith (ANQM, Louis Chaboillez minutes). He moved from Detroit to Sandwich, on the Canadian side of the Detroit River, shortly after his marriage to Cécile Descomps (Descomptes) dit Labadie at Assumption Church, Sandwich, on 20 September 1803. Jean-Baptiste Piquette, a Detroit silversmith, was a witness to their marriage (BHC). He was buried at Assumption Church, Sandwich, on 17 August 1825. His wife was remarried to Benjamin-François Chevrier on 28 January 1826, and was buried at Assumption Church on 18 January 1838 (BHC).

Lagrave was active largely in the making of Indian trade silver, as attested by contemporary documents. An entry in the account book of John McGregor, merchant of Sandwich, for 23 March 1808, credits him with making silver Indian trade ornaments valued at over £31–4.792 small brooches, 15 large brooches, 13 ear wheels, and 12 large ear wheels (FMM).

AUGUSTIN LAGRAVE

29 Teaspoon, ca. 1810–20

MEASUREMENTS
Length 14.8 cm. (5$\frac{13}{16}$ in.); weight 10.5 gm. (7 dwt.)

MARK
Script AL in oval (stamped once on underside of handle)

CONDITION
Very worn; repaired by William L. Siebert, Northville, Mi., 19 May 1951

PROVENANCE
Made for Labadie family (Louis Descomps dit Labadie[?], born 1788), Detroit; collection Laura Labadie, Detroit; collection Francis W. Robinson, Grosse Pointe Farms, Mi.; gift to DIA 23 July 1973.

Gift of Mr. and Mrs. Francis W. Robinson (75.36)

DESCRIPTION
Fiddle pattern: narrow shank of thin; flat stem gradually expanding to broad-shouldered upper section with turned-down and slightly squared end; ovoid bowl with pointed end.

94

Fig. 38

This spoon combines two patterns which were popular at the beginning of the nineteenth century, the fiddle and the coffin handles. The latter, with squared, coffin-shaped handle end, was a distinctly American type and was used only briefly after 1800. The coffin shape of this spoon has been somewhat modified, and the corners are only slightly clipped. Aside from the pattern, the thin gauge of the silver is also typically American and suggests that this spoon was made sometime after Augustin Lagrave's arrival in Detroit.

The earliest teaspoons in Quebec date from the second half of the eighteenth century, although coffee spoons do occur much earlier because of the preference of the early French population for coffee.

The attribution of the maker's mark (fig. 38) was made by Francis W. Robinson. According to Miss Laura Labadie, this teaspoon was made for the Labadie family; family tradition held that it was made by Antoine Lagrave (1735–1834) of Montreal. Antoine died in Detroit on 11 August 1834 and was buried at Assumption Church, Sandwich, on the same day (BHC). He was a master carter (carrier) in Montreal (ANQM, Joseph Papineau minutes, 15 March 1787). The style of the spoon, which is relatively late, as well as its distinctly American character, makes an attribution to Antoine unlikely, but his son Augustin is known to have been an active silversmith, and he is the probable maker. Augustin was also related by marriage to the Labadie family: his wife was Cécile Descomps dit Labadie. Cécile's brother, Louis, was the great-grandfather of Miss Laura Labadie on both the maternal and paternal sides (FWR). This teaspoon is the only known surviving piece by Augustin Lagrave.

95

Paul Lambert dit Saint-Paul

Quebec City

1691 or 1703(?)–1749

Paul Lambert was born in the parish of Sainte-Catherine, in Arras, capital of the province of Artois, France. The son of Paul Lambert and Thérèse Stuart(?), the year of his birth is variously given as 1691 or 1703 (Derome, p. 93). He probably served his apprenticeship in his native town. He arrived in Quebec City about 1728 or 1729 as one of a group of naval officers and artisans whom Monseigneur Dosquet had recruited for the colony from Flanders and neighboring provinces (Morisset, ''L'orfèvre Lambert,'' p. 14). On 30 August 1729, he married Marie-Françoise Laberge in Quebec City. They had nine children and from 1733 on resided on rue Sault-au-Matelot. Lambert's wife died on 28 November 1747, and he married Marie-Marguerite Maillou on 19 February 1748. She was the niece of Jean Maillou, a Quebec architect whose son Joseph (1708–1794), a silversmith, is thought to have apprenticed under Lambert. Joseph Maillou was employed by Lambert from about 1730 until his master's death on 25 November 1749. Lambert bequeathed his silversmithing tools to his youngest living son, François, then thirteen years old. Although François began an apprenticeship under his father, it is not known whether he ever became an active silversmith (Derome, pp. 93–97).

Paul Lambert was the most prolific Quebec silversmith of the first half of the eighteenth century and the first to earn his livelihood entirely through his craft. Although he received numerous church commissions, his chief clientele was the petite bourgeoisie, whose requirements were usually limited to écuelles, tumblers, and flatware, as the wealthier gentlemen-bourgeois preferred to order from the more prestigious Parisian workshops.

PAUL LAMBERT DIT SAINT-PAUL

30 Tumbler, ca. 1740–49

MEASUREMENTS
Height 5.5 cm. (2$\frac{3}{16}$ in.); diameter of mouth 7.3 cm. (2$\frac{7}{8}$ in.); weight 69.9 cm. (2 oz. 5 dwt.)

MARK
PL under fleur-de-lis and above five-pointed star, in shaped cartouche (stamped once underneath) (fig. 39)

INSCRIPTION
Stamped below outer rim, L. DVBORD

CONDITION
Slight denting around bottom edge; repair to lip

PROVENANCE
Possibly made for Louis Dubord dit Clermont, Les Grondines, Que., and Sandwich, Ont.; H. Baron, Montreal; DIA purchase 10 June 1949.

Fig. 39

BIBLIOGRAPHY
Fox, *Traditional Arts*, no. 38 (ill.).

EXHIBITION
Windsor 1975

City Appropriation (acc. no. 49.406)

DESCRIPTION
Bell-shaped tumbler with flared and fluted lip, of small dimensions and relatively thick silver construction.

No. 30

The tumbler, also known as a *gobelet de roquille,* or *petit gobelet,* was a popular early drinking vessel and follows a rather traditional formula. Used for spirits, it was rarely made in Canada after 1800. Its rather small size contrasts with the wider tumbler and larger beakers which were popular in the American colonies. Lambert produced numerous tumblers and, at the time of his death, had on hand orders for seventeen (Morisset, *Lambert,* p. 102, n.2).

The fashioning of a tumbler was a rather simple task. It was partially raised in a hollow of the silversmith's tree-trunk, then inverted over a stake and hammered to achieve the vertical sides and rounded bottom. The rim was thickened and strengthened by caulking, or hammering down, on the top edge. As final decorative touches, a burin was used to gouge two flutes at the rim and a line was incised below.

This tumbler contains about two liquid ounces, and apparently at the time of his death Lambert specialized in four or five basic tumbler sizes. Four sizes can be calculated from the weight in silver of each tumbler recorded in his estate inventory. On the basis of weight (they are approximate, in old French weights), each tumbler falls into one of four groups: 2 oz. 2 gros (68.21 gm.), 2 oz. 4 gros (75.78 gm.), 2 oz. 6 gros (83.36 gm.), and 3 oz. (90.94 gm.). This tumbler is the smallest of these. Lambert's tool inventory also mentions five *boulottes à gobelets,* which Gérard Morisset describes as *estampes en fer tendre* ("stamps in soft iron") (*ibid.,* pp. 94–102 and n. 7). These are probably the stakes with ball or rounded heads which were used in making tumblers. Although a silversmith could make different-sized tumblers from a single small stake, his work would be much easier if he had a number of stakes to fit the various standard tumbler sizes. The fact that Lambert had five *boulottes* for tumblers suggests that he may have made an additional tumbler size as well.

Because of their standardized form, tumblers cannot be dated precisely, and their provenance is usually equally difficult to establish. An important clue on this particular example is the inscription, which may represent the original owner. There is only one person of the name Dubord and with the initial "L" who can be identified in Canadian records of the first seven decades of the eighteenth century. He is Louis Dubord dit Clermont, son of Charles Lafontaine dit Clermont and Marie Rollet of Les Grondines, Quebec. The only definite date which can be assigned to him is that of his marriage to Louise Bouron at Sainte Anne's Church, Detroit, 5 October 1744 (BHC). They resided at the "South Shore of Detroit," today known as Sandwich. They had numerous children, but the last record of any person of that name to be found in the Detroit area is Louise Dubord dit Clermont, daughter of Louis, who married Guillaume Daperon at Assumption Church, Sandwich, on 16 June 1768 (BHC, RBMB, Sainte Anne, Detroit). Louis Dubord is not mentioned in the Detroit census of 23 January 1768, which included the "South Shore" (WLC, Gage Papers, "The Census of All the Inhabitants of Detroit made by Philip Dejean in the Year 1768 on January 23rd," Turnbull to Gage, 23 February 1768), which suggests that Dubord returned to Quebec with his family before 1768. Many of the French settlers in the Detroit region did so after the British conquest of New France in 1759. Louis Dubord was born sometime after 1712, and it is probable that he commissioned this tumbler shortly before or after his marriage in 1744, thus the date 1740–49.

Dubord is not the only person with Detroit connections to have ordered silver from Paul Lambert. In 1749 Claude Gouin (or Goün) ordered an écuelle with a plate, a dozen *couverts* (a *couvert* is a spoon and a fork), and a serving spoon (Morisset, *Lambert,* pp. 98, 99). Gouin was living in Detroit as early as 13 January 1742, when he married Marie-Joseph Cuillerier. Under the French government of Detroit, he was the royal surveyor as well as a lieutenant in the militia. He died at Detroit on 29 May 1776 (BHC, RBMB, Sainte Anne, Detroit).

Jean-François Landron

Montreal and Quebec City

1686–ca. 1760

Born at Quebec City on 27 December 1686, Jean-François Landron was the son of Étienne Landron and Élizabeth de Chauvigny (Derome, p. 98). His father was a pastry cook who became wealthy as a baker, trader, and shipowner. His mother was a Chauvigny de la Chevrotière, related to the Vaudreuils and other noble families of New France (Carrier, p. 2). He is first mentioned as a silversmith on 22 November 1719, when he married Marie-Anne Bergeron in Montreal (Tanguay, 5:127). In 1721 he was in Quebec City, where the account books of Notre-Dame Basilica indicate that he made a chrismatory. He also made a censer for that church in 1724, for which he signed the following receipt: "I have received from M. Grandmeny, churchwarden in charge of the parish church of Notre-Dame de Quebec, the sum of 138 livres, 12 sols, 6 deniers, half of the 277 livres, 5 sols, which is due me for the fashioning and silver supplied for a censer which I have made for the aforesaid church at Quebec this 30th of June 1724" (Derome, pp. 101–2). Although he was an active silversmith, it appears that Landron's chief occupation was that of a merchant and ship-owner: he is known to have owned at least three ships (Cauchon and Juneau, p. 348). On 10 July 1739, his wife was godmother at the baptism of Amable Maillou (1739–1808), who became a silversmith and was active in Montreal and Detroit (ANQQ, RBMB, Notre-Dame de Québec). In the Quebec City census of 1744, Landron is listed as living on rue Notre-Dame (Derome, pp. 104–5). On 26 July 1756, he became the godfather of Françoise Poisset. Landron died sometime between that date and the year 1760 (Cauchon and Juneau, p. 348).

31 Ciborium, ca. 1719; bowl replaced ca. 1790 by Robert Cruickshank

MEASUREMENTS

Height 25.7 cm. (10⅛ in.); diameter of bowl 13.2 cm. (5¾ in.); diameter of base 14.1 cm. (5⁹⁄₁₆ in.); weight 545.2 gm. (17 oz. 11 dwt.)

MARKS

Script RC in shaped outline (stamped twice on outside bezel of bowl); also remnant of mark with star?) on dome of foot (fig. 40)

CONDITION

Stem and foot, originally separable, brazed solid; cross finial and threaded rod of bowl replaced; small crescent-shaped repair above knop; minor repairs to stem and foot

PROVENANCE

Church of Saint-Eustache, Deux-Montagnes County (near Montreal), until the late 1960s (letter of André Racine, curé); Jean Octeau, Montreal; DIA purchase 11 May 1969.

BIBLIOGRAPHY

Fox, "Liturgical Silver," pp. 100–101, 103, fig. 3; Fox, "French Canadian Silver," pp. 77–78, fig. 1; Fox, *Traditional Arts,* no. 36.

EXHIBITION

Windsor 1975

K. T. Keller Fund (acc. no. 69.264)

DESCRIPTION

Plain raised bowl with vertical sides, bottom with rounded edge and slightly convex center, applied molding below rim forming bezel, and disc with threaded rod brazed to bottom; the interiors of both bowl and cover are mercury-gilt. The cover is a compressed pear form with a rather prominent dome capped by an applied gadrooned surround and a screwed Maltese cross finial.

The baluster stem has two collar knops in the form of flared and beaded flanges; the knop itself is an inverted and slightly compressed pyriform with a lower chased laurel frieze. Above the knop is a two-part spool with a fillet applied to the joining; the lower spool is actually one piece with the upper knop, and both are demarcated by an intervening chased line; thus the knop is raised in two parts, the upper shoulder and lower spool and the lower knop, which are seamed together midway up the shoulder. The upper spool is also raised; the collars are wrought and punched, and the fillet and upper cylinder (threaded internally) are swaged and seamed. The foot is domed and splayed, and the upper dome has a small everted rim which separates it from the lower acanthus border. This border was stamped and then brazed to the upper dome. A thin seamed ring of silver is brazed underneath the outer edge of the foot.

Evidently this piece may be electroplated, as the silver readings are above 99 percent silver except for the cup, which is 94.66 percent. The probability of electroplating is supported by subsequent readings taken after polishing and scraping. Progressively reduced readings were obtained, the lowest being 97.39 percent silver, indicating that the readings do not reflect the true metallic composition (see Appendix II). It was not an uncommon practice to electroplate old pieces, and this was usually done in the present century.

The foot and stem of this ciborium were formerly attributed to Roland Paradis (ca. 1696–1754) of Montreal. However, stylistically they differ markedly from the general character of Paradis' ciboria, as evidenced in a piece made for the church of Saint-Charles, Lachenaie, in 1739 (Traquair, pl. 12a). With a wide shallow bowl and ball knop, that piece was rendered after an archaic seventeenth-century design. In contrast, the basic design of the Detroit ciborium is later and is found on French ciboria at the turn of the eighteenth century, although it is a slightly later colonial rendition.

The entire ciborium, except for the bowl, appears to be the work of Jean-François Landron, although his mark has probably been effaced as a result of wear. The design of the foot is almost identical with that of all Landron's known ciboria, monstrances, and chalices (Trudel, nos. 127, 128, 130 [ill.]). This similarity extends even to the finest details of the basal acanthus leaf borders, suggesting that Landron always used a standard type of leaf puncheon(s) or die(s). Also, the basal flange of Landron's pieces was formed by simply everting the edge of the domed part of the foot rather than applying a separate band, as was commonplace among his contemporaries.

Most early Quebec silversmiths did not practice their craft as a full-time occupation but engaged in other activities as well, and Landron was no exception. Such silversmiths did not need a wide range of tools, and what they used they usually made themselves or imported. A silversmith such as Landron would have only a few decorative puncheons, swages, and dies. Although essentially French in design,

Fig. 40

Fig. 41. Jean-François Landron, monstrance, detail. H. 38.5 cm. Musée du Québec, acc. no. A.70.15.0.

the ornament from these tools would bear his own imprint, arising largely from his limitations and preferences as a craftsman, especially if he made the tools himself. Thus most early ornamented silver has motifs characteristic of individual silversmiths, and these motifs provide an invaluable guide in the identification of unmarked pieces.

The knop of this ciborium has a distinctive shape and in basic outline recalls that on Landron's monstrance at the Musée du Québec (fig. 41). It lacks the gadrooning of the Quebec monstrance, but both have a similar stylized laurel leaf frieze. The leaves of both have a chased outline and ribs and an upper punched fringe. The beaded collar knops are also similar, as are fillets above the knops. As each early Canadian silversmith usually worked in a very individual manner, in spite of attempts at imitation of French pieces, it is possible to conclude that the stem and foot of this ciborium were made by Landron.

The cover is by his hand as well. The outline of the lip and flange of the cover is very similar to that on another smaller ciborium by Landron, formerly at the Episcopal Palace in Quebec City (fig. 42). There is a slight difference in the extent of the protuberance and curvature of the domed cover, but this is simply the result of an adjustment of the design to compensate for the difference in size. Microscopic analysis of the brazed seams of the cover reveals a splattering of minute beads of brazing solder, indicating that Landron had not yet mastered the brazing technique. This splattering is also found on the foot and stem, but not on the bowl.

The bowl was replaced around 1790 by Robert Cruickshank, whose mark is found twice on the outer bezel. A later date is also indicated by its relatively flat bottom, which contrasts with the almost hemispherical shape preferred in the early eighteenth century. The threaded rod with

102

disc brazed underneath the bowl is a modern replacement; the cross finial was probably added in the nineteenth century. Otherwise, it appears that this vessel was made by Landron. Partial refashioning of damaged or worn church vessels was a frequent occurrence.

The repairs of Cruickshank must have been made before 1800 because Pierre Huguet is the only silversmith recorded as making silver for the church of Saint-Eustache at the turn of the nineteenth century. The only entry in the parish account books referring to a ciborium was made in 1808: "For the purchase of a ciborium and chalice, etc., 824 livres" (IBC, Saint-Eustache [Deux-Montagnes] file, Grand livre de la fabrique, fols. 31, 34). Apparently these were made by Huguet.

This is probably the earliest of three surviving ciboria by Landron, a third being at the church of Saint-Charles Borromée, Charlesbourg. The latter was almost completely refashioned by Laurent Amiot in 1809, and the foot which bears Landron's mark is all that remains of the original ciborium (IBC, Charlesbourg file, photo A-8). The Detroit piece is probably early, as suggested by the unskilled handling of the brazing technique and the somewhat unsophisticated design. The proportions are awkward, and the design lacks cohesiveness, as evident in the wide, relatively flattened foot, and the tall, slender stem. This piece originates in the Montreal area, which provides another valuable dating clue. Landron practiced his craft in Quebec City from 1721 until about 1750. Prior to this he worked for a short period in Montreal, about 1719. This ciborium probably dates from this early period, which would make it the earliest known church piece by Landron and one of the earliest extant pieces of church silver made in Quebec. However, it was not originally made for the church of Saint-Eustache, as that church was not founded until 1768 (Magnan, p. 355).

Fig. 42. Jean-François Landron, ciborium. H. 20.9 cm. National Gallery of Canada, Ottawa, acc. no. 14,834.

Paul Morand

Montreal

1784–1854

Paul Morand was the last important silversmith of the Montreal area. The son of Laurent Morand, a blacksmith, and Pélagie Massue, he was born at Blainsville, near Montreal, 4 April 1784. The following day he was baptized Joseph at the church of Saint-Eustache. His parents later called him Hippolyte, which he shortened to Paul. On 28 April 1802, he was apprenticed to Pierre Huguet dit Latour I for three years. In addition to board, lodging, and training in the rudiments of the craft, he received an annual salary of 100 livres (Morisset, "Morand," p. 29). Upon completion of his apprenticeship, he continued in the Huguet workshop as a companion for an undetermined period but certainly not after the death of the elder Huguet in 1817. He then established his own workshop, which in 1819 was located at 1 rue Saint-Vincent (Doige, p. 142), and after 1831 at rue Saint-Amable (Langdon, *Canadian Silversmiths,* p. 103). After the death of his chief rival, Salomon Marion, on 31 October 1830, he became the leading maker of ecclesiastical plate in the Montreal area until his death on 11 July 1854. His widow was Marie-Anne Dufresne, whom he married on 29 September 1845 (Morisset, "Morand," p. 30).

PAUL MORAND

32 Chalice, ca. 1825

MEASUREMENTS
Height 20.6 cm. (8⅛ in.); diameter of cup 7.1 cm. (2¹³⁄₁₆ in.); diameter of base 11.8 cm. (4⅝ in.); weight 284.2 gm. (9 oz. 4 dwt.)

MARK
PM in rectangle (stamped four times under foot) (fig. 43)

CONDITION
Minor repairs to foot

PROVENANCE
H. Baron, Montreal; DIA purchase 30 October 1957.

BIBLIOGRAPHY
DIA, *Tannahill,* pp. 68, 69 (ill.); Fox, *Traditional Arts,* no. 48.

EXHIBITION
Windsor 1975

Gift of Robert H. Tannahill (acc. no. 57.143)

DESCRIPTION
Three separable parts, cup, baluster stem, and foot, fashioned and assembled in a manner similar to No. 25. The plain bell-shaped cup has a flared lip and gilt interior. The baluster stem has an upper cylinder, a chased dentiled collar knop, a two-part spool with mid-molding, an urn-shaped knop with chased stepped shoulder and lower molding, a molded and flared cylinder, and a chased dentiled collar knop. The foot is domed and splayed, with a dentiled flange, *cyma reversa* molding, and a strengthening band; a small cross on a hillock is engraved on the front of the dome.

Morand's small liturgical vessels made for the use of missionaries, like this chalice, are particularly delightful. It serves as a companion piece to a small ciborium by Morand also at Detroit (No. 33). At first glance, the overall design looks like an imitation of Laurent Amiot (cf. fig. 24); how-

Fig. 43

Fig. 44. Paul Morand, chalice, H. 17.8 cm. Henry Birks Collection, Montreal, acc. no. C.472.

ever, closer examination reveals the overweighing influence of Pierre Huguet, with only the plain urn-shaped knop borrowed from Amiot. Recognizable are the dentiled collars of the stem and the dentiled basal flange. The *cyma reversa* basal molding is almost always employed by Huguet (cf. the chalice shown in IBC, Ile-Perrot file, photo B-6), whereas Amiot preferred the cavetto. The treatment of these elements is the same as on the Huguet ciborium, No. 25. This design was repeated by Morand on other occasions, as in another missionary chalice formerly in the collection of Chanoine (Canon) Silvestre of Montreal (IBC, Paul Morand file, photo A-5) and a chalice in the Henry Birks Collection (fig. 44). These chalices are identical except for fillets above and below the knops of the last two and the cavetto basal molding of the Birks chalice, which also relates it closely to Amiot's work. Morand frequently borrowed forms and motifs from other silversmiths, as did his immediate predecessors. He imitated works not only by Huguet and his contemporaries but also by early silversmiths such as Paul Lambert (DIA, *French in America,* p. 70 [ill.]). These are not necessarily servile and exacting reproductions, as Morand often makes slight alterations to the designs and thus adds his own personal touch. This process can be seen in the Detroit chalice.

Chalices in general, and the small missionary ones in particular, did not always belong to a church; they were often the property of an individual priest. Upon his death, his chalice was sometimes left to a church, but usually it was transferred to a central repository such as the chancery of a diocese or to the mother-house, if the priest belonged to a religious order. These chalices were then dispensed to other priests, especially those newly ordained. Because of this constant transferral to new owners, the provenance of most missionary chalices is almost impossible to trace.

33   Ciborium, ca. 1825–50

MEASUREMENTS
Height 20.5 cm. (8¹⁄₁₆ in.); diameter of bowl 8 cm. (3⅛ in.); diameter of base
10.5 cm. (4⅛ in.); weight 263.7 gm. (8 oz. 9 dwt.)

MARKS
PM in rectangle; lion passant and sovereign's head, each in shaped cartouche (each stamped once under foot) (fig. 45)

CONDITION
Cross finial rebrazed to cover; also slight repairs to cover

PROVENANCE
H. Baron, Montreal; DIA purchase 30 October 1957.

BIBLIOGRAPHY
DIA, *Tannahill,* pp. 2 (ill.), 68.

Gift of Robert H. Tannahill (acc. no. 57.144)

DESCRIPTION
Four separable parts, cover, bowl, baluster stem, and foot, fashioned and
assembled as seen with No. 25. The domed cover is a plain compressed
pear form with a molded flange and a molded vertical lip applied to the
rim. A small cast half-orb, with an applied flat cross finial, is brazed to the
central protuberance of the cover. The inside of the bowl and the cover are
electro-gilt. The raised bowl has vertical sides, a rounded bottom edge, and
an applied molding below the rim forming a bezel. The baluster stem has
two dentiled collar knops, an upper molded cylinder, a two-part spool with
chased beaded band, an archaic inverted pyriform knop with prominent
stepped shoulder, two finely reeded moldings, and a flared molded cylinder. The plain domed foot has a dentiled flange projecting over a high *cyma
reversa* molding, and an outer strengthening band.

Fig. 45

A small-scale reproduction of a basic design for ciboria used
by Pierre Huguet (No. 25), the small size indicates its
functions as a portable missionary ciborium. Morand's only
design innovation is the omission of the gadrooning, usually
found on Huguet's knops. The dependence of Morand on
Huguet in both the design and construction of this piece,
suggests that it may have been produced early in his career,
when his master's influence was strongest. The design also
recalls Cruickshank's ciboria, and the use of dentils harks
back to the work of the Parisian Guillaume Loir (No. 16).

The electro-gilding of the bowl and cover raises some
question as to the date of this piece. Gilding was performed
by the mercury process until the 1850s, when it was
gradually replaced by electro-gilding. If this ciborium was
originally electro-gilt, it undoubtedly dates from the close of
Morand's career, about 1850–54 but the cover shows signs of
repair, and in all probability this piece was regilt later in the
century.

PAUL MORAND

34 Snuff Box, ca. 1835–50

MEASUREMENTS
Height 1.4 cm. ($\frac{9}{16}$ in.); length 5.9 cm. ($2\frac{5}{16}$ in.); width 3.9 cm. ($1\frac{9}{16}$ in.);
weight 56.95 gm. (1 oz. 17 dwt.)

MARK
PM in rectangle (stamped once under lid and once inside bottom)

CONDITION
Thumb grip rebrazed

PROVENANCE
From the Montreal area; S. Breitman Antiques Ltd., Westmount
(Montreal); DIA purchase 30 October 1974.

BIBLIOGRAPHY
Fox, *Traditional Arts,* no. 49.

EXHIBITION
Windsor 1975

Elizabeth, Allan, and Warren Shelden Fund (acc. no. 74.119)

DESCRIPTION
Rectangular box with scalloped edges and gilt interior; lid connected at
back by a five-part pinned hinge. The lid has a central incised medallion
with double outline on a diapered ground, and a scalloped edge molded in
reverse curves at the front and back and in curved segments at the sides and
angles. Three small incurving sides are brazed to the edge of the lid; the
back has three applied hinge cylinders; a small bracket thumb grip is
applied to the front. The box has incurving sides formed from a single strip
seamed at the right front angle and brazed to the bottom. A bezel is applied
to the front and sides and a hinge plate with two cylinders to the back. The
bottom is plain except for an incised outline at the scalloped edge.

In eighteenth-century France and England small silver
boxes were extremely popular. They served as compact con-
tainers for a variety of items ranging from sweetmeats,
seals, jewels, pills, and salve to snuff. They were made in
many shapes and were often exquisitely decorated. This
fashion spread to Canada in the eighteenth century, where
snuff boxes were particularly popular. Their use began to
decline by the middle of the nineteenth century, and they
became increasingly rarer thereafter.

109

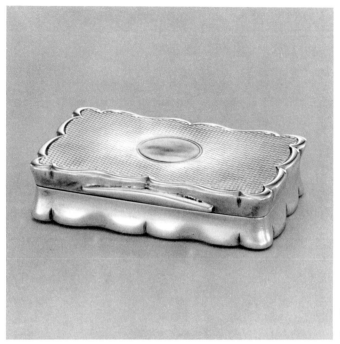

No. 34a

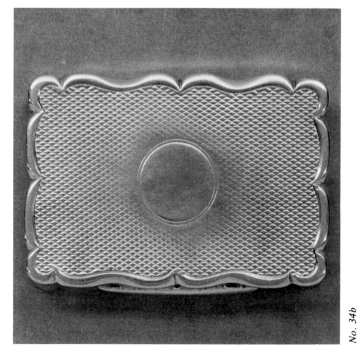

No. 34b

Fig. 46

The form of this snuff box, rectangular with rounded corners, was popular at the beginning of the nineteenth century. It was a late Neoclassic development, and related Neoclassic decorative motifs are seen in the medallion and diaperwork of the lid. The scrolled edges of the lid, however, betray a Neo-Rococo influence and give this box a somewhat eclectic character. The combining of these two styles dates the box after about 1835.

The attribution of this piece is somewhat uncertain as there is no gold trace in the elemental composition and no precedent for the maker's mark (fig. 46) (the former point is discussed in Appendix II). The maker's mark was not struck from the same punch as the marks on the two previous pieces by Morand (see figs. 43 and 45, where the marks are unquestionably those of Morand). In the past, there has been a great deal of confusion regarding Paul Morand's marks and those of his contemporary, Paul Morin (1775–1816+) of Quebec City, as apparently both men used the initials PM enclosed in a rectangle, and many pieces by Morand have been incorrectly ascribed to Morin. However, many of these pieces can be sorted out solely on stylistic grounds, as Morand was indebted to Huguet for many of his designs, while Morin imitated those of his master, Laurent Amiot. With this as a basis and with a knowledge of the provenance of some of these pieces, it can be deduced that Morand had at least three variant marks. These are illustrated in Langdon, *Marks,* p. 53, where two are assigned to Morin. At present it cannot be determined whether the mark on this snuff box was a fourth variation used by Morand. If it does not belong to him, it may be Morin's or even a forgery: in fact, with further study, this piece may prove to have been made in the late nineteenth century.

Roland Paradis

Quebec City and Montreal

ca. 1696–1754

Born in Paris about 1696, where, presumably he was trained, Roland Paradis emigrated to Canada sometime before his marriage to Marie-Angélique Boivin at Quebec City on 3 February 1728. Their marriage contract of 22 January 1728 describes him as: "Sieur Roland Parady (*sic*), a merchant silversmith living in this city, son of Claude Paradis, also a merchant silversmith in the city of Paris on the Pont au Change, parish of Saint-Jacques de la Boucherie, and of Geneviève Cuizy, his spouse, his father and mother" (Derome, p. 151). The Pont au Change was the famed silversmith's quarter in Paris. According to the same document, Roland's brother, Louis, was a tailor in Quebec City. About 1732 Roland moved to Montreal, resided on rue Saint-Joseph after 1741, and resided on rue Saint-Jean-Baptiste after 1748. On 27 October 1748 he engaged Jean-Baptiste Legu dit La Noue (1737–1762+), who was twelve years old, as his special assistant for a term of ten years. About this time Charles-François Delique (ca. 1723–1780+) also entered his workshop. A relative of Paradis' and a trained silversmith newly arrived from Paris, Charles-François was the son of Charles-François Delique, a Parisian silversmith. When Roland died in Montreal on 28 April 1754, he left his tools and workshop to Charles-François (*ibid.*, pp. 52, 111, 152–57).

Paradis was the leading Montreal silversmith of the second quarter of the eighteenth century and, next to Paul Lambert of Quebec City, the most productive silversmith of New France. More than forty of his pieces are known to survive; they were made for Quebec City and Trois-Rivières, as well as the Montreal area. There is even evidence that he had an occasional commission from Detroit, as did Paul Lambert.

ROLAND PARADIS

35 Écuelle, ca. 1730

MEASUREMENTS
Height 4.6 cm. (1$\frac{13}{16}$ in.); diameter 16.8 cm. (6$\frac{5}{8}$ in.); length 28.9 cm. (11$\frac{3}{8}$ in.); weight 421.2 gm. (13 oz. 11 dwt.)

MARK
RP crowned in shaped cartouche (stamped four times underneath) (fig. 47)

INSCRIPTION
Stamped on outer rim, MORISSO (Morisseau)

PROVENANCE
Hubert family, of the Hubert seigneurie near Quebec City; transferred to a collateral line, the Neilsons; descended to Gordon A. Neilson, Quebec City; H. Baron, Montreal; Paul Gouin, Montreal; DIA purchase 14 October 1946.

BIBLIOGRAPHY
DIA, *French Canada*, p. 37 (no. 133), pl. 18; Morisset, "L'orfèvrerie canadienne," fig. 3; Morisset, "Paradis," pp. 26 (ill.), 31; Oglesby, fig. 151; DIA, *French in America*, p. 68, no. 107 (ill.); Morisset, "Roland Paradis," p. 440, fig. 2; Langdon, *Canadian Silversmiths*, pl. 33; DIA, *Tannahill*, p. 68; Trudel, p. 216, no. 150 (ill.); Fox, *Traditional Arts*, no. 39.

EXHIBITIONS
Detroit 1946; Detroit 1951b; Dearborn 1967; Ottawa 1974; Windsor 1975

Gift of Robert H. Tannahill (acc. no. 46.350)

DESCRIPTION
Low flat-bottomed bowl with two ear-lug handles. The schematized triangular handles are outlined by plain moldings and have knob tips; a small palmette or shell motif is at the center of each on a plain ground. The handles were cast in a sand mold and then brazed below the rim of the bowl; a bracket or thickening bar is applied underneath each handle at the join with the bowl.

The design of this écuelle is drawn from late seventeenth-century France. Paradis produced many écuelles, all of this type, with slight variations only in the handles. He seemed to prefer two types of handles, one with a border molding and palmette, cast as a single unit, the other a plain lug cut from a sheet of silver, with applied cast palmette (Trudel, no. 151 [ill.]; cf. No. 6). The overall design of these vessels differs little from that of other écuelles of the first half of the eighteenth century in New France. For example, the Detroit écuelle resembles one by Paul Lambert at Hôtel-Dieu, Quebec City (*ibid.*, no. 107 [ill.]).

This écuelle was owned by the Hubert family and possibly by Charles-François Hubert (1680–1754) or his son Jacques-François (1716–1758), both seigneurs of the Hubert seigneurie (manor). Charles-François was keeper of the Quebec City prisons; Jacques-François was a baker in the same city. Jean-François, son of Jacques-François, was the curé of Assumption Church, Sandwich, and missionary to the Hurons from 1781 to 1784. He was consecrated coadjutor bishop of Quebec in 1786 and became bishop in 1788 (Roy, "Hubert," pp. 756–59).

Fig. 47

On 6 January 1797, Marie-Ursule Hubert, granddaughter of Jacques-François, married John Neilson (1776–1848), and it was possibly through this marriage that the Neilsons acquired the Hubert écuelle. The Neilsons also succeeded to the seigneurial estates of the Huberts, which they retained until relatively recently (*ibid.*, p. 758). John Neilson, the first of the Neilsons, was a Scot who arrived at Quebec City in 1790 and became editor of *La Gazette de Québec* in 1796, perhaps the most important newspaper in Lower Canada (Quebec) in the early nineteenth century. He was an ardent and vociferous spokesman for the French Canadian cause. In 1818 he was elected to the House of Assembly of Lower Canada as the member for Quebec County, a seat he held until 1834. He was re-elected in 1841, when he became speaker of the Assembly, a position he retained until his death on 1 February 1848.

No. 35

Jean-Baptiste Piquette

Montreal and Detroit

1779–1813

According to the register of Notre-Dame Church in Montreal, Jean-Baptiste was baptized on 21 January 1779, son of Amable Piquet (Piquette) and Marie-Joseph LeDuc (ANQM). He probably served his apprenticeship in Montreal and then moved to Detroit sometime prior to 1803. On 20 September 1803, he witnessed the marriage of Augustin Lagrave, a Montreal-trained silversmith, and Cécile Descomps dit Labadie at Assumption Church, Sandwich, across the river from Sainte Anne's Church, Detroit (BHC). That same year he entered into partnership with the French-trained silversmith Pierre-Jean Desnoyers, who had settled in Detroit in 1796. Their joint enterprise ceased with the Detroit fire of 11 June 1805 (Robinson, "Detroit Silversmith," p. 23). On 27 March 1806 Jean-Louis Monet was bound to Piquette for six years, during which time he was to learn the craft of silversmith. This contract was revoked on 1 August 1809 (BHC, J.-B. Piquette Papers). Piquette was primarily a maker of silver ornaments for the Indian trade and numerous surviving contracts indicate that he made them in considerable quantity.

He married Eléonore Descomps dit Labadie, sister of Augustin Lagrave's wife, on 31 January 1809 at Assumption Church (BHC). Lagrave was a witness. Two sons were born of this union, both of whom became silversmiths active in Detroit: Jean-Baptiste, born 29 September 1809, died 24 August 1851, and Charles, born 4 February 1813 and died 9 August 1859. Piquette's career was prematurely terminated with his death on 24 April 1813, when he was only thirty-four years old (BHC, RBMB, Sainte Anne, Detroit).

JEAN-BAPTISTE PIQUETTE

36 Écuelle, ca. 1805

MEASUREMENTS
Height 5 cm. (2 in.); diameter 16.8 cm. ($6\frac{5}{8}$ in.); length 29.2 cm. ($11\frac{1}{2}$ in.); weight 433.8 gm. (13 oz. 18 dwt.)

MARKS
BP, PIQUETE, each in rectangle (stamped once underneath) (fig. 48)

PROVENANCE
Made for Bâby family (possible Jean-Baptiste Bâby) of Detroit and Sandwich; descended to Bâby family members in Montreal area; John L. Russell, Montreal; DIA purchase 9 January 1961.

BIBLIOGRAPHY
Robinson, "Detroit Silversmith," p. 23 (ill.); *Antiques* 87 (1965):323 (ill.); Simmons, p. 22 (ill.); Fox, "French Canadian Silver," p. 80, fig. 7.

EXHIBITIONS
Dearborn 1964; Grosse Pointe Woods 1973; Grosse Pointe Woods 1975

Elizabeth and Allan Shelden Fund (acc. no. 61.7)

DESCRIPTION
Shallow, flat-bottomed bowl with slightly convex sides and contracted rim. The two symmetrically opposed crown handles were cast separately and then brazed just below the rim.

No. 36

Fig. 48

Fig. 49

The design of the handles (fig. 49) is not that of the traditional French Canadian écuelle. Rather, it is an adaptation of a pewter handle type known as a crown handle which is found on eighteenth-century pewter porringers in New England. The crown handle has an openwork decoration with a crown (actually a viscount's coronet), small pellets representing jewels, and scrolled foliate supporters (Robinson, "Detroit Silversmith," p. 23; Raymond, pp. 144–49).

The shape of the bowl is also unusual for an écuelle. Its bulging sides and contracted rim are typical of the eighteenth-century American porringer and its English counterpart, the bleeding bowl. Apparently Piquette copied a pewter porringer (which would have had one handle) and merely added a second handle. By such means he succeeded in translating an American vessel into one of uniquely French Canadian design.

This écuelle is the largest surviving piece by Piquette, and the finest. It may have been made for Jean-Baptiste Bâby (1770–1852) of Sandwich, brother and business partner of the Honorable Jacques Bâby. There is also a spoon (acc. no. 54.283) in the Detroit collection by the Detroit silversmith François-Paul Malcher (1751–1810) which is engraved "JBB," for Jean-Baptiste Bâby. This spoon came from the same descendants of the Bâby family as the Piquette écuelle.

37   Tablespoon, ca. 1800

MEASUREMENTS
Length 23.5 cm. (9¼ in.); weight 57.5 gm. (1 oz. 17 dwt.)

MARK
PIQUETE in rectangle (stamped once on underside of handle) (fig. 50)

INSCRIPTION
Engraved on upper front of handle, CC (Christian Clemens)

CONDITION
Far end of handle has crack indicating tendency to break; end of bowl worn

PROVENANCE
Made for Christian Clemens, Mt. Clemens, Mi. (FWR); gift of his great-granddaughter to DIA 8 December 1952.

BIBLIOGRAPHY
DIA, *French in America,* p. 201, no. 540; Robinson, "Early Detroit," p. 8; Robinson, "Detroit Silversmith," p. 23.

EXHIBITIONS
Detroit 1951b; Dearborn 1964

Gift of Miss Rebecca L. Crittenden (acc. no. 52.240)

DESCRIPTION
Old English pattern: slender, relatively flat shank gradually expanding to rounded, turned-down end; ovoid bowl and rounded drop at back juncture of bowl and stem.

Fig. 50

Christian Clemens, the founder of Mt. Clemens, Michigan, was born at Horsham, Montgomery County, Pennsylvania, 31 January 1768. He came to Detroit about 1795 and began a distinguished career as a manufacturer of leather, a distiller of whiskey, a probate judge of Macomb County, a trustee of the University of Michigan, a colonel in the Michigan militia, and a participant in the organization of several railroads. In 1803 he married Elizabeth Tallmadge Allen. He died at Mt. Clemens on 25 August 1844 (FWR).

38   Holy Water Stoup and Aspergill, after ca. 1855

MEASUREMENTS
Stoup: height including handle 27.4 cm. (10$\frac{13}{16}$ in.); height 19.1 cm. (7$\frac{1}{2}$ in.); diameter of shoulder 19 cm. (7$\frac{7}{16}$ in.); diameter of base 12.8 cm. (5$\frac{1}{16}$ in.); weight 883.8 gm. (28 oz. 8 dwt.). *Aspergill* (sprinkler): length 26.9 cm. (10$\frac{9}{16}$ in.); weight 127.5 gm. (4 oz. 2 dwt.)

MARK
HP in oriflamme cartouche (stamped twice under flange of mouth)

CONDITION
Several small dents on shoulder of stoup; gilding (probably nineteenth-century) removed 10 September 1969, resulting in a slightly dull patina

PROVENANCE
Church of Saint-Octave de Métis, Matane County, Que.; S. Breitman Antiques Ltd., Westmount (Montreal); Jean Octeau, Montreal; DIA purchase 28 January 1970.

BIBLIOGRAPHY
BDIA 48 (1969):39 (ill.); Fox, "Liturgical Silver," p. 103, fig. 9.

Gift of Mrs. Allan Shelden (acc. nos. 69.300 a, b)

DESCRIPTION
Urn-shaped bucket with arched handle and high domed foot. The raised bucket has an upper swaged cavetto collar with an applied chased dentiled flange and vertical rim band with horizontal lip. The shoulder and lower bucket are chased with identical acanthus friezes on a matte and punched ground; these friezes are separated by a narrow ribbed band between two plain, highly burnished bands.

The circular domed foot is splayed and stepped, with a plain stem, beading, gadrooning, and molded edge. This section might be spun; the gadrooning is chased; small brazed shot balls form the beading. A strengthening band is applied inside the basal rim. The plain, cylindrical, arched handle has a molded ball knop at its apex. The handle is fashioned like that on the Huguet stoup (No. 26). The horizontal handle ends are held in sockets of two quatrefoil brackets brazed to the rim of the mouth.

The cylindrical shaft of the aspergill tapers to a spherical perforated head. The shaft is pinched at midpoint; a small ring at the circular backplate contains a large suspension ring.

The attribution of this stoup to Henri Polonceau (1766–1828) is no longer acceptable. Polonceau was a relatively obscure silversmith, jeweler, and clockmaker, active both in LaPrairie and Montreal, and only about a dozen minor pieces, largely flatware and cruet trays, are attributed to him. Each of these pieces bears one of three variant marks with the initials HP in a rectangular frame. Two of these marks are illustrated in Traquair, p. 63; one has a triangular indentation at the left side of the frame similar to the mark on the Detroit stoup (fig. 51), and the other lacks a border on the left side. Another smaller mark, with a triangular indentation at both the top and the bottom of the frame, occurs on a spoon at the Musée du Québec. In view of his apparent small production it is inconceivable that Polonceau would have had other punches. But how is the mark on the Detroit stoup to be explained, especially as it is almost identical with the first-mentioned mark of Polonceau?

It is most unusual that two almost identical marks, with the same initials and distinctive frame, would be used by two different silversmiths. Moreover, there are no known marks by other Quebec silversmiths with a triangular indentation of this sort in the frame. The Detroit mark may be a modern attempt to reproduce a well-known mark of Polonceau or may belong to another silversmith. What is certain is that if this mark is authentic, it dates from the middle to late nineteenth century. The design of this stoup first appeared in Quebec about a decade after Polonceau's death; an identical mark occurs on a chalice, in a private collection, which dates from the late nineteenth century. Other "HP" marks occur on nineteenth-century Quebec silver, again chiefly flatware. One of these is ascribed to

No. 38

Henry Peacock, active in Montreal from about 1847 to 1890 (Langdon, *Canadian Silversmiths,* p. 113 [ill.]); the others are unidentified. Attempts have been made to identify the mark on the Detroit stoup with Peacock, but he is an unlikely choice, as he was largely a dealer in watches, clocks, and jewelry (see the *Canada Directory* for 1851, p. 224).

Essentially Empire in spirit, this design is nineteenth-century French, which presupposes a source in either France or Quebec. The elemental composition of the bucket, which averages about 92 percent silver, would seem to exclude the former (see Appendix II). After 1797 two silver standards were followed in France, one at 80 percent and the other at 95 percent (Helft, p. 330). If this piece were French, it should be within the range of one of these standards. On the other hand, the silver content and gold and lead traces here are typical of much nineteenth-century Quebec silver (see p. 154). The handle may be a twentieth-century replacement, as suggested by the low percentages of trace elements and the extreme differential in the silver content of the handle, at 97.4 percent, and the rest of the stoup.

Aspects of this design are also found in the work of two important Quebec silversmiths, François Ranvoyzé and Laurent Amiot. These same decorative motifs, in the same arrangement, are found on a stoup by Ranvoyzé at the church of Saint-Joseph, Deschambault (*Ranvoyzé,* no. 6 [ill.]). The urn shape of the bucket recalls Amiot's stoups (Langdon, *Canadian Silversmiths,* pl. 10), as well as the burner bowl of his later censers and his sanctuary lamps. However, the design has a more immediate reference in the work of François Sasseville, who made an almost identical piece for the church of Saint-Louis, Kamouraska, in 1839 (IBC, Kamouraska file, photo B-10; the Sasseville stoup was damaged by fire in 1914 and shortly thereafter, was partially refashioned by the silversmith Arsène Belleville). Sasseville does omit the textural effects found on the Detroit piece, but, in general, his stoup dates this design to about

Fig. 51

the mid-nineteenth century. In fact, Sasseville's copy raises the question, as yet unresolvable, of whether the Detroit stoup could be his as well, or perhaps by one of his successors, such as Pierre Lespérance.

The provenance of this stoup is also uncertain. It is said to have been made for the church of Saint-Pierre du Sud, Montmagny County, but is not mentioned in the church account books. Moreover, the number of surviving vessels by early silversmiths at that church would seem to rule out that possibility. All the surviving silver bears the mark of Laurent Amiot except for two small French sanctuary lamps of 1752, a chalice and a chrismatory by François Ranvoyzé of 1783, a ciborium by Joseph Sasseville of about 1820, and a pyx by François Sasseville of about 1840. The items by Amiot include a baptismal ewer, a chalice, a censer, an incense-boat, a holy water stoup, a monstrance, a lavabo, and a sanctuary lamp, all made between 1790 and 1837 (Morisset, "Saint-Pierre," p. 50).

According to Gérard Morisset, the church possessed a second holy water stoup in 1837, as implied by the following entry in the second parish account book: "29 June 1837, in the course of his pastoral visit Monseigneur Signay ordered to be obtained: ... A holy water stoup and aspergill for everyday use ... A lavabo for the purification of the fingers" (IBC, Saint-Pierre du Sud [Montmagny] file, Livre de comptes, II [1783–1845]). The qualification "for everyday use" infers that there was another stoup for use on Sundays and holy days. A later entry that year contains the same implication: "For the repair of the aspergill, 5 shillings." Laurent Amiot made the lavabo that same year, along with all silver known to have been ordered by that church for the previous thirty-seven years except the ciborium by Joseph Sasseville, and so he undoubtedly made the new stoup, which is probably the one presently at the church. It is unlikely that the first stoup mentioned is the one at Detroit; it is equally unlikely that the church would commission a third stoup later in the century.

The Detroit stoup became the property of the church of Saint-Octave de Métis, in the remote Gaspé region, which was founded in 1855 (Magnan, p. 603). The first caretaker pastor of that church, Jean-Baptiste Duguay, in a letter of 17 September 1855 to Archbishop Pierre-Flavien Turgeon of Quebec outlined the many needs of the new parish, including sacred vessels. He wrote: "I have the honor of acknowledging the receipt of your letter dated the 13th of this month in which you request information for your future pastor of Métis. It is much easier to tell you what there is than what there is not. ... There is hardly a sacred vessel of any form" (Métis, p. 123). The Detroit stoup was probably made for this church sometime after this was written.

Dominique Riopelle

Detroit

1787–1859

Dominique was born at Detroit on 20 September 1787, the son of Ambroise Riopel (Riopelle) and Thérèse Campau, who were married at Detroit on 24 November 1766. His father originally came from Ange-Gardien, Quebec, where he was born on 3 March 1738. Dominique married Colette Gouin at Sainte Anne's Church, Detroit, on 26 January 1818 (BHC). According to family tradition, he was an active silversmith, but little work bearing his mark survives. Early nineteenth-century documents indicate that his brother Pierre (1772–1811) was also a silversmith (FMM, Account Book of John McGregor, 10 and 12 September 1808). Dominique died at Detroit on 17 May 1859 (BHC, RBMB, Sainte Anne, Detroit).

DOMINIQUE RIOPELLE

39 Pair of Tablespoons, ca. 1825

MEASUREMENTS
Length of right spoon 23.1 cm. (9⅛ in.); weight in right spoon 65.2 gm. (2 oz. 2 dwt.). Length of left spoon 23.1 cm. (9⅛ in.); weight of left spoon 66.7 gm. (2 oz. 3 dwt.)

MARKS
Script DR in oval; D. REOPELLE in engrailed cartouche (each stamped once on underside of both handles)

INSCRIPTIONS
Engraved on upper front of handles, AG; stamped on reverse, LLT (Louis LaTouche)

PROVENANCE
Louis LaTouche, Saint-Henri de Lauzon, Que.; descended to his daughter, Virgine LaTouche, and then to her great-nieces, two spinsters named Marceau, all of Saint-Henri de Lauzon; acquired from Marceau heirs by a Quebec City dealer; collection Louis Carrier, Sainte-Anne de Bellevue, Que. (FWR); DIA purchase 9 October 1950.

BIBLIOGRAPHY
DIA, *French in America*, p. 201, nos. 541 and 542.

EXHIBITIONS
Detroit 1951a; Detroit 1951b; Grosse Pointe Woods 1973

Gift of Mrs. Lillian Henkel Haass (acc. nos. 50.131, 50.132)

DESCRIPTION
Fiddle pattern: chamfered shank of stem with two spurs above bowl, expanding to broad, shouldered upper section with rounded, turned-down end; ovoid bowl with slightly pointed end and small, incised, V-shaped drop at back juncture of bowl and stem.

This pair is part of a set of six spoons. Two others, formerly in the collection of Louis Carrier, are presently at the Musée du Québec (IBC, Louis Carrier file, photo WW-2). The original owner, represented by the initials AG, has not been identified. The spoons were subsequently acquired by Louis LaTouche, either a son or nephew of Louis LaTouche and Thérèse Fougère dit Champagne, of Repentigny, Quebec, where LaTouche was born. According to family tradition, Louis LaTouche was living in the *pays d'en haut,* or Upper Great Lakes region, when he acquired these spoons in Detroit. Upon returning to Quebec, he settled at Saint-Henri de Lauzon, a village eight miles from Lévis, and it was there that he had the spoons stamped with his initials by an itinerant silversmith. The set was passed down intact among his descendants until it was sold and divided in 1950.

Although the fiddle pattern was popular in both Canada and the United States during the early nineteenth century, these spoons combine minor features which can be classified as being either distinctly American or French Canadian and thus are related to the slightly earlier écuelle by Jean-Baptiste Piquette (No. 36). The thick gauge of the silver is typical of Quebec silversmiths, but the V-shaped drop and the placement of the engraving lengthwise on the handle are typically American. Quebec silversmiths generally retained the rounded drop and usually placed engraving crosswise on the handle, design aspects retained from eighteenth-century practice (cf. No. 13).

Mention should be made of the spelling of ''Reopelle'' in the maker's mark (fig. 52). This is a typical distortion of a French Canadian name like Riopel or Riopelle. Often the holder of the name distorted it himself in an attempt to make sure that an English-speaking community would approximate the correct French pronunciation of his name. Other variants of this name occur in contemporary documents of the Detroit and Sandwich area, such as ''Reaopel'' and ''Reopell'' (FWR).

Fig. 52

125

40 Gorget, ca. 1810–25

MEASUREMENTS
Length 13.5 cm. (5 5/16 in.); width 4 cm. (1 9/16 in.); weight 18.1 gm. (12 dwt.)

MARK
Script DR (the D is partially effaced), in oval (stamped once on front)

PROVENANCE
Indians of Village-des-Hurons (Lorette), near Quebec City; collection Louis Carrier, Sainte-Anne de Bellevue, Que.; collection Lucille Carrier; DIA purchase 13 May 1964.

BIBLIOGRAPHY
DIA, *French Canada*, p. 41, no. 169; DIA, *French in America*, p. 201, no. 543.

EXHIBITIONS
Detroit 1946; Detroit 1951b; Windsor 1953; Dearborn 1967

Gift of Robert H. Tannahill (acc. no. 64.87)

DESCRIPTION
Convex crescent with rolled edge and cut from thin sheet silver. A large stylized tortoise is engraved with short strokes on the central portion. Because the first letter of the maker's mark is somewhat obliterated (fig. 53), the attribution of this piece has been somewhat uncertain. Louis Carrier originally assigned it to "DR," or Dominique Rousseau (1755–1825), a silversmith active in Montreal, Detroit, and Mackinac, but in 1946 he reassigned it to Pierre Riopelle of Detroit (DIA, *French Canada,* no. 169). In 1952 he attributed it to Dominique Riopelle (Riopel), younger brother of Pierre (DIA, *French in America,* no. 543). This mark is identical with Riopelle's small mark on the preceding two tablespoons (fig. 52).

Fig. 53

The tortoise motif was the totem of the Tortoise tribe of Huron Indians, for whom this gorget was originally made. This type of ornament was suspended from the neck and served as a badge of honor. It was derived from a similar ornament worn by officers in the British army, which itself was a last remnant of the armor worn by medieval knights (Robinson, "Indian Trade Silver," p. 10).

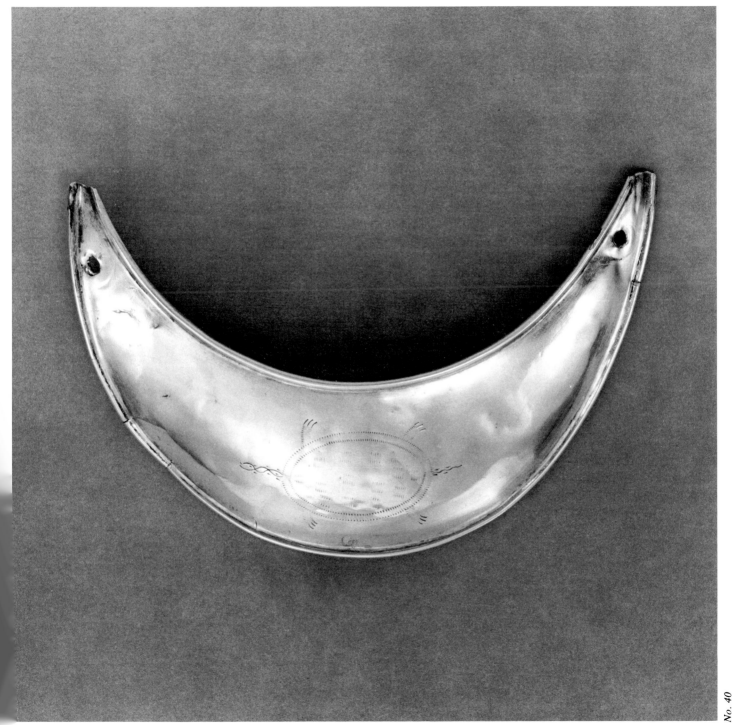

Louis Robitaille

Quebec City and Detroit

1765–1821+

Louis, son of Pierre Robitaille and Geneviève Parant (Parent), was born at Loretteville, Quebec, in 1765. He married Louise, daughter of George Munro and Judith Lacroix, on 21 April 1789 at Quebec City (Tanguay, 7:13). His sister, Geneviève, married the Quebec City silversmith Jean-Nicolas Amiot (1750–1821), brother of Laurent Amiot (*ibid.*). On 12 May 1790, Paul Morin was apprenticed to Louis Robitaille for six years to learn the trade of silversmith; this contract was broken within a year. In 1791 Robitaille worked at 25 rue Sous le Fort, Quebec City, and in 1792 he was at 12 Côte de la Montagne (Langdon, *Canadian Silversmiths,* p. 120). By 1794 he was in Detroit; he and his wife were godparents at the baptism of François, son of François Gouin and Angélique Godet, at Sainte Anne's Church on 1 May 1794 (BHC). In the Campau family papers, there is an order from Louis to the merchant Joseph Campau for a pound of gunpowder, dated 6 and 18 June 1794 (BHC). In the same year he is mentioned as "Louis Robitaille, silversmith" in the business papers of John Askin, another Detroit merchant (BHC).

His daughter Victoire was born at Detroit in 1795 and was baptized 28 days later on 20 October at Sainte Anne's Church (BHC). She died at Lévis, Quebec, on 18 October 1796 (Langdon, *Canadian Silversmiths,* p. 120). It is not known how long Robitaille remained in Detroit; however, he continued to make silver for the Detroit area. In the inventory book (1819–1821) of Angus Mackintosh, merchant and Indian trader at Sandwich, he is included among

the list of debtors: "Louis Robitaille, silversmith, £1/6/0 (BHC)."

LOUIS ROBITAILLE

41   Tablespoon, ca. 1800–1810

MEASUREMENTS
Length 21 cm. (8¼ in.); weight 52.1 gm. (1 oz. 13 dwt.)

MARKS
LR in rectangle (stamped twice on underside of handle); lion passant in shaped cartouche (stamped once on underside of handle) (fig. 54)

CONDITION
End of bowl worn

PROVENANCE
Philippe family, Detroit; collection James O. Keene, Birmingham, Mi.; gift to DIA 26 June 1961.

Gift of Mr. and Mrs. James O. Keene (acc. no. 61.188)

DESCRIPTION
Old English pattern: slender, lightly chamfered shank gradually expanding to rounded, turned-down end with lip; ovoid bowl, and rounded drop at back juncture of bowl and stem.

This tablespoon is one of the few surviving pieces attributed to Louis Robitaille. It comes from the Philippe family of Quebec and Detroit. The original owner was possibly John (or Jean) Philippe, who came from Quebec and had a house and store (built in 1836) at the corner of Orleans and Atwater Streets, Detroit (FWR).

Fig. 54

129

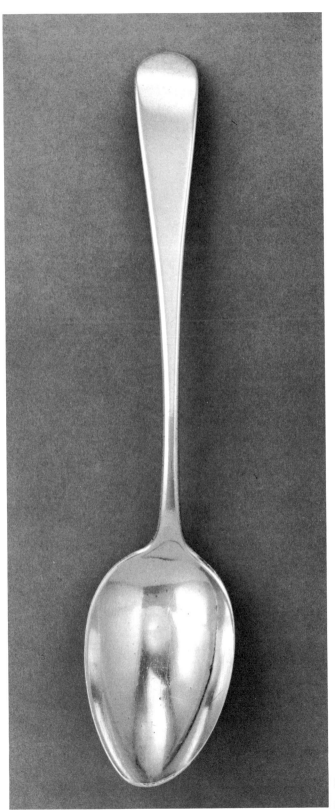

François Sasseville

Quebec City

1797–1864

Many details of François Sasseville's background remain obscure, although his contemporaries called him the most important Quebec silversmith of the mid-nineteenth century. He was born at La Pocatière (or Sainte-Anne de la Pocatière, formerly Sainte-Anne-du-Sud), Quebec, on 30 January 1797, the son of Joseph Sasseville and Geneviève Roy. His father was a tavern-keeper and merchant in La Pocatière, as well as a boat captain, fisherman, and navigator. François' early years were spent accompanying his father on fishing expeditions to Gaspé. He signed a petition which his father and forty-five associates presented to James Monk, administrator of Lower Canada, on 29 February 1820, for a grant of land at Cap Chat (Morisset, "Sasseville," p. 51). Sometime later, he proceeded to Quebec City, where he was apprenticed under Laurent Amiot (Carrier, p. 12). His older brother, Joseph, was already an active silversmith there.

After completing his apprenticeship, François continued as a companion in the Amiot workshop and eventually succeeded to the business upon his master's death in 1839. He immediately became the unrivaled master silversmith of the Quebec City area. His production was prolific, although he was faced with rugged competition from imported French and English silver. Numerous contemporary newspaper accounts testify to the ubiquitous appeal of his work. An 1846 entry from the *Journal de Québec* states: "Monsieur Sasseville, the only craftsman of his type which we have in Quebec, has just completed a superb silver ciborium and the magnificent craftsmanship should be admired in Europe as well as in Canada" (Morisset, "Sasseville," p. 52).

In the *Canada Directory* (p. 333) for 1851, his workshop is listed at 17 Côte de la Montagne, and in the *Canada Directory* for 1857–58 (p. 606) it is at 7 Côte du Palais. Sometime before 1857 he established a partnership with his nephew, Pierre Lespérance, a former companion. This partnership lasted until Sasseville's death on 28 February 1864, when Lespérance took over his workshop. The assets of his estate amounted to about twenty-five thousand dollars, a considerable sum for the time. A third of the estate went to Lespérance and the remainder to other relatives and local religious communities. Sasseville also left his apprentice, Ambroise Lafrance, the sum of one hundred dollars (Morisset, "Sasseville," p. 53). Although Lespérance and Lafrance were capable artisans, Sasseville was the last outstanding silversmith of the Quebec tradition.

130

FRANÇOIS SASSEVILLE

42 Monstrance, ca. 1850

MEASUREMENTS
Height 66.4 cm. (26⅛ in.); width of sunburst 34.4 cm. (13⁹⁄₁₆ in.); base 19.3 cm. (7⅝ in.) × 14.3 cm. (5⅝ in.); weight 1,762 gm. (56 oz. 13 dwt.)

MARK
FS in oval (stamped once on upper verso of cross finial) (fig. 55)

CONDITION
Lowest cluster of rays on right repaired; tips of some rays broken off

PROVENANCE
Reportedly church of Saint-Denis de Kamouraska, Kamouraska County, Que.; S. Breitman Antiques Ltd., Westmount (Montreal); DIA purchase 18 June 1970.

BIBLIOGRAPHY
Fox, "Liturgical Silver," p. 103, fig. 11; Fox, "French Canadian Silver," p. 80, fig. 8; Fox, *Traditional Arts,* no. 50.

EXHIBITIONS
Grosse Pointe Woods 1975; Windsor 1975

Elizabeth, Allan, and Warren Shelden Fund (acc. no. 70. 650)

DESCRIPTION
Monstrance of three separate units with threaded connectors: pedestal, baluster stem, and *soleil* or sunburst. Elevated on four foliate scroll feet, the pedestal has a lower plain band, a *cyma reversa* molding with laurel and acanthus frieze, and a dado with a plain band framing its four sides and creating four separate panels. Above a torus cornice with chased oval motif is a rectangular domed section with a frieze similar to that of the lower molding. The four feet, possibly fashioned by hammering into a negative die, are reinforced with an applied back-plate and are brazed to the four corners of the pedestal. Each side of the lower band, the molding, the dado, and the torus is fashioned separately; the sides of each section are brazed at the corners; and each section is brazed together. The upper dome is raised, its corners are shaped, and it is applied to the torus. A disc with an inserted threaded sleeve is applied at the center of the dome and receives the threaded rod of the stem.

The panels of the dado contain iconographical symbols common to monstrances of the period. On the front panel, a lamb, cross, and book are superimposed on an altar with lancet arches. This grouping is embossed separately, attached to the pedestal with a screw and nut, and surrounded by the clouds and flat rays of the panel. Both side panels contain an identical pruned grapevine with three bunches of grapes; the back panel contains an equilateral triangle surrounded by clouds and rays. All ornament, including the stem and sunburst, is generously embossed, chased, and punched, providing rich and varied surface textures.

The baluster stem has a large urn-shaped knop with two projecting winged angel heads and, below, a smaller boss with a band of laurel leaves and a small reeded molding. The knop and lower boss are raised. Each angel head is formed by hammering into a mold, in two halves, and then seamed and applied. Above the knop, the stem is a vertically seamed cylinder with chased reeds terminating at a large nailhead, or faceted, band below the sunburst. Beyond this band the reeds metamorphose into ears of wheat, and the upper stem appears as a bound sheaf of wheat. At the front of the sheaf are four repoussé bunches of grapes; grapes are repeated among the ears of wheat on the lower part of sunburst; the wheat motif is reproduced alone on the reverse of the sunburst. Two scrolls in an almost heart-shaped device frame a vine laden with grapes on the front and back of the knop.

From the bottom of the knop upward, including the sunburst, the monstrance has a diamond-shaped outline. At the center of the diamond shape is a large circular aperture surrounded by a narrow reeded frame. The aperture has two panes of glass with an intervening gold ring forming an enclosed transparent receptacle; the back pane has an outer rim, a three-part pinned hinge, and an adjacent pinned latch. This receptacle is grooved for the reception of a *lunula,* or lunette, consisting of two panes of glass in a hinged frame of gold, with a lower hooked finger grip.

The large cloudband framing device surrounding the lunette is connected to the stem by a recessed threaded rod in the faceted band. This frame is fashioned in two halves, including the faceted band, and is seamed at the sides. The clouds are embossed, chased, and incised, and the winged angel heads are hammered into a mold and applied. The front has two angel heads flanking the lunette and two above.

Eleven stamped clusters of flat overlapping rays are inserted into openings at the edge of both sides of the cloudband. The original bilateral symmetry of the clusters is disrupted, as the tips of some rays are broken off. The sunburst is surmounted by an inserted flat cross, the front of which is covered with hearts, shells, and a *cross patée* at the crossing and a shell at the end of each arm.

The monstrance is an expositional receptacle for a large Eucharistic wafer which is placed in the lunette at the center of the sunburst. The whole is designed so that the wafer is elevated vertically and thus can be easily viewed by the devotees. The monstrance resembles a reliquary, and the wafer is exhibited in the manner of a relic.

This monstrance is typically mid-nineteenth century in its monumental proportions and abundant decoration. Eighteenth-century monstrances are generally smaller and less ornate. The large rectangular pedestal did not become standard for Canadian monstrances until the early

131

nineteenth century and was used frequently by Sasseville (fig. 56). In the preceding century, an oval domed foot was preferred.

There are two facets to Sasseville's oeuvre, those works in which he pedantically followed Laurent Amiot and those in which he developed a more personal style based on contemporary French imports. This monstrance belongs to the latter category (cf. Grandjean, fig. 12, 3). It is also related to the later works of Amiot and of Sasseville's Quebec contemporaries such as Paul Morand, which often show the influence of nineteenth-century French designs (Ignatieff, p. 149 [ill.]; Langdon, *Canadian Silversmiths,* pl. 7).

Overall, this monstrance is an effusive ornamental extravaganza, overladen with appropriate religious symbols. The accumulation of ears of wheat and grapes symbolizes the two species of the Eucharist, the bread and the wine; the rays of the sunburst represent the glory of the divine presence in the Eucharist. On the front panel of the pedestal, the lamb, or *agnus dei,* symbolizes Christ, and the cross and altar represent the sacrificial aspects of Christ's crucifixion. The book refers to Christ and to the book of the seven seals which is found in the New Testament (Revelation 5–6). Altogether they symbolize Christ's Passion and the mystery of Christian salvation as embodied in the Eucharist exhibited in the monstrance. They are intended to evoke the spirit of the words of Saint John: "Behold the Lamb of God, who taketh away the sin of the world" (John 1:29). On the back panel of the pedestal, the equilateral triangle symbolizes the Holy Trinity. This triangle also contains the Hebrew letters for Jehovah, or God the Father.

This monstrance originates from the parish of Saint-Denis de Kamouraska, which was established canonically in 1833. The first permanent chapel was built in 1839, but it had no resident priest until the arrival of Édouard Quertier in 1841. This monstrance was probably commissioned sometime after this date. It should be noted that Laurent Amiot,

Fig. 55

Fig. 56. François Sasseville, monstrance. H. 45.7 cm. National Gallery of Canada, Ottawa, acc. no. 16,869.

Sasseville's master, executed a monstrance for the neighboring church of Saint-Louis, Kamouraska, in 1833–34. Although destroyed in a fire of 1914, tradition holds that it was ordered to be made in the old French manner of the eighteenth century, and thus was probably unlike this example by Sasseville (Paradis and Morisset, pp. 278–80, 340).

Fig. 57

FRANÇOIS SASSEVILLE

43 Ciborium, ca. 1852

MEASUREMENTS
Height 26.6 cm. (10½ in.); diameter of bowl 11.3 cm. (4⅞ in.); diameter of base 12.2 cm. (4¹³⁄₁₆ in.); weight 681.7 gm. (21 oz. 18 dwt.)

MARK
FS in oval (stamped twice under foot) (fig. 57)

INSCRIPTION
Scratched under foot, "1852 Alain curé de Bonaventure 1852"

PROVENANCE
Church of Saint-Bonaventure d'Hamilton, Bonaventure County, Gaspé; S. Breitman Antiques Ltd., Westmount (Montreal); DIA purchase 6 March 1974.

BIBLIOGRAPHY
BDIA 53 (1974):57, 84 (ill.).

Elizabeth, Allan, and Warren Shelden Fund (acc. no. 74.3)

DESCRIPTION
Almost identical with the ciborium by Laurent Amiot at Detroit (No. 7) except for the absence of a calyx and slight variations in construction. The four parts are connected in the usual manner. The plain raised bowl has a domed cover with a riveted pedestal and cross finial. A vertical seamed band, forming the lip, is applied to the outside of the down-turned edge of the cover, and a plain horizontal flange is applied over the join. The bowl, with an electro-gilt interior, has an applied bead below the rim forming a bezel. The baluster stem has a plain inverted pyriform knop and a torus collar knop; the knop is fashioned like that of the Amiot ciborium, possibly cast and turned. The upper swaged and seamed spool has an upper applied disc encircling an inserted threaded sleeve. A small vent hole in the disc is not found on the Amiot piece. The lower raised bellform contains a projecting threaded connector, now a rod of small diameter with an enlarged threaded head rather than a seamed and threaded cylinder, as seen in previous ciboria.

The collar knop and the domed and splayed foot are constructed like Amiot's ciborium. The narrow everted edge of the dome has an applied vertical flange projecting over an outer cavetto molding with an applied strengthening band. Shallow fluted and raying strapwork flares out over the upper dome.

For a discussion of the electro-gilding of the bowl, see Appendix II (p. 155). Sasseville frequently copied Amiot's designs, and he repeated this particular design, with minute variations, on numerous occasions (No. 44). Similar ciboria

Fig. 58. François Sasseville, ciborium. H. 27.3 cm. National Gallery of Canada, Ottawa, acc. no. 16,870.

by Sasseville are found at the National Gallery of Canada (fig. 58), and the church of Saint-Charles des Grondines, Portneuf County. The latter was made in 1840 at a cost of 20 louis, which provides a relative value for these ciboria (IBC, Les Grondines file, photo C-6).

The name Alain, inscribed under the foot, refers to abbé Jean-Louis Allain (1813–1863), and "Bonaventure" is the church of Saint-Bonaventure d'Hamilton, Bonaventure. Allain was the first resident parish priest of that church; he served there from 1837 to 1863 (Allaire, p. 9; Magnan, p. 259). The date 1852 may be the year in which the ciborium was acquired.

134

FRANÇOIS SASSEVILLE

44 Ciborium, ca. 1855

MEASUREMENTS
Height 25.7 cm. (10⅛ in.); diameter of bowl 11.8 cm. (4⅝ in.); diameter of base 12.4 cm. (4⅞ in.); weight 677.8 gm. (21 oz. 16 dwt.)

MARK
FS in oval (stamped three times under foot) (fig. 59)

PROVENANCE
Cathedral of Saint-Jean-Baptiste de Nicolet, Nicolet County, Que.; S. Brietman Antiques Ltd., Westmount (Montreal); DIA purchase 11 September 1970.

BIBLIOGRAPHY
Fox, "Liturgical Silver," p. 103, fig. 8.

Robert H. Tannahill and Robert H. Tannahill Memorial Funds (acc. no. 70.719)

DESCRIPTION
Identical with the previous ciborium by Sasseville (No. 43) except for the surface gilding, the lower flared cylinder of the baluster stem, which replaces the bellform, and the more elaborate strapwork of the foot. The strapwork is identical with that on the Amiot ciborium at Detroit (No. 7).

Fig. 59

Sasseville deviates slightly from Amiot's formula in the use of allover gilding. The taste for extensive gilding was stimulated by contemporary silver imported from France, as well as the introduction of a newly developed technique in gilding known as electro-gilding. This new technique was used in the Sasseville workshop in Quebec as early as the 1850s. Before that time all gilding was done by the mercury process (see Appendix II). Electro-gilding of this piece, which is confirmed by the elemental analysis, is indicated by the anemic yellow cast and the thinness of the gilt surface, most of which has worn through to the silver. Gilding with mercury has an orange-yellow cast and is quite durable. If the vessel was not gilded by Sasseville, or by Pierre Lespérance, who was responsible for most of the electro-gilding in the Sasseville workshop, it was probably done in the late nineteenth century, when the extensive gilding of church vessels was especially popular. Gilding not only enriched the visual effect, but also obviated the need for frequent polishing of the surface, as gold does not tarnish.

Sasseville received other commissions from the church of Saint-Jean-Baptiste de Nicolet, which was elevated to cathedral status in 1885 (Magnan, pp. 463–64), including a censer, again in the manner of Amiot which is still in its possession.

FRANÇOIS SASSEVILLE

45 Dessert Fork, ca. 1845

MEASUREMENTS
Length 16.8 cm. (6⅝ in.); weight 45.8 gm. (1 oz. 9 dwt.)

MARKS
FS in rectangular cartouche (stamped twice on underside of handle); QUEBEC in rectangle (stamped once on underside of handle) (fig. 60)

INSCRIPTION
Engraved on upper front of handle, wheat sheaf surmounted by horizontal sword

PROVENANCE
Gift to DIA 29 July 1969.

Gift of Jean Octeau (acc. no. 69.526)

DESCRIPTION
Fiddle pattern: lightly chamfered shank of stem with two lower, right-angled spurs gradually expanding to broad-shouldered upper section with rounded, turned-up end and slight medial ridge; four tines, rectangular in section, taper to pointed tips.

Fig. 60

In the French Canadian manner, the gauge of the silver is thick, and the fork relatively heavy. The wheat sheaf and sword on the front of the handle probably represent an unidentified family crest, although the wheat sheaf was also a common decorative motif on contemporary American fiddle pattern flatware. The four-tine dessert fork appeared in Quebec, as in the United States, in the early nineteenth century. The dessert fork was a smaller version of the dinner fork (No. 15), and was usually about 6.5 inches long (16.5 cm.), slightly shorter than the dessert spoon (see No. 19).

Joseph Sasseville

Quebec City and La Pocatière

1790–1837

Joseph, older brother of François Sasseville, was born at La Pocatière on 14 April 1790. He married Françoise Laflèche at Quebec City on 5 November 1811 (FWR, notes of Louis Carrier). Little is known of his silversmithing career. According to John Langdon, he had a shop on 34 rue Saint-Paul, Quebec City, in 1822; in the census of 1831 he is recorded as being on the same street (Traquair, p. 43). From his surviving works, he is known to have made liturgical silver, flatware, and Indian trade silver. His mark (IS, in an oval) is sometimes found in conjunction with that of James Orkney (active 1791–1826) of Quebec City (IO, in a rectangle), and they may have been partners for a period (Langdon, *Canadian Silversmiths,* pp. 110, 123). According to Louis Carrier, Joseph also worked in La Pocatière prior to his death there on 3 September 1837 (FWR).

JOSEPH SASSEVILLE

46 Salt Spoon, ca. 1825

MEASUREMENTS
Length 9.8 cm. (3⅞ in.); weight 7.85 gm. (5 dwt.)

MARK
IS in oval (stamped once on underside of handle) (fig. 61)

PROVENANCE
H. Baron, Montreal; collection Francis W. Robinson, Grosse Pointe Farms, Mi.; gift to DIA 23 July 1975.

Gift of Mr. and Mrs. Francis W. Robinson (75.39)

DESCRIPTION
Fiddle pattern: shank of lightly chamfered stem has two right-angled spurs above bowl, gradually expanding to broad-shouldered upper section with rounded, turned-down end and short medial ridge underneath; deep oval bowl and small rounded drop at back juncture of bowl and stem.

This spoon is indistinguishable from American examples of the same period. Salt spoons were found in several shapes, all miniature versions of ordinary spoons, shovels, and ladles. The ladle shape can often be distinguished from the mustard spoon only by the length of the handle: the latter had a slightly longer and narrower handle.

Fig. 61

141

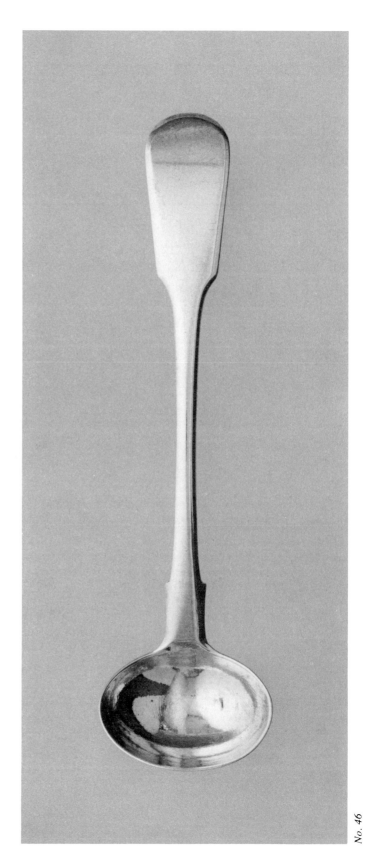

Joseph (or Jonas) Schindler

Quebec City, Mackinac, Detroit, and Montreal

Active 1763–1792

Son of Joseph Schindler and Marguerite Gaspar, residents of the town of Saint-Nicolas in Glarus, Switzerland (Tanguay 7:152), Schindler first appears in Quebec City in 1763 as an "engineer of mathematical instruments" (ANQQ, Claude Louet minutes, 12 November 1763). At his marriage to Marie-Geneviève Maranda at Quebec City on 17 May 1764, he is mentioned as a silversmith (Carrier, pp. 7–8). In 1766 Louis Huguet dit Latour was engaged to him as an apprentice silversmith for six years (see p. 83). On 9 February of the following year, Jean-Nicolas Amiot, brother of Laurent Amiot, silversmith, was apprenticed to Schindler for four years (ANQQ, Claude Louet minutes). In the spring of 1775, Schindler joined Guillaume Monforton in outfitting a trading expedition to Mackinac (Michilimackinac), where he was active making Indian trade silver (ANQQ, Jean-Antoine Panet minutes, 21, 23, and 25 March 1775). In 1777, he was in Detroit with another apprentice, Michel Forton, also from Quebec City. On 8 August of that year, he was tried before Philippe Dejean, a justice of the peace, for "having made, sold, and offered to sale, base metal mixed with silver." In his defense Schindler declared that he was "not a good judge of the quality of silver, having never served an apprenticeship to the silversmith, or any other business." Although acquitted by the jury, Lieutenant-Governor Henry Hamilton had him drummed out of town for exercising a craft in which he had never received training (*Remembrancer,* pp. 188–91). Schindler was in Montreal in 1778, but it is not known whether he took up permanent residence there at that time or whether he returned to Quebec City. On 27 May 1784 (*GQ*), he advertised the sale of a house in Lower Town, Quebec City. By the mid-1780s he was established in Montreal, where he had a thriving business in domestic and ecclesiastical silver, as well as in silver ornaments for the Indian trade. Schindler engaged his last apprentice, Joseph Normandeau, on 29 September 1791 (FWR, notes of Louis Carrier); he died on 19 November 1792. He was buried from Christ Church, Montreal, on 21 November (ANQM). His wife continued his workshop, largely occupied with making Indian ornaments, until her own death on 11 January 1803 (ANQM, RBMB, Notre-Dame de Montréal, 13 January 1803).

Fig. 62

JOSEPH SCHINDLER

47 Ladle, ca. 1785

MEASUREMENTS
Length 32.1 cm. (12$\frac{11}{16}$ in.); diameter of bowl 9.3 cm. (3$\frac{11}{16}$ in.); weight 190 gm. (6 oz. 2 dwt.)

MARK
IS in rectangle (stamped four times on underside of handle) (fig. 62)

PROVENANCE
Bâby family, Lachine, Que. (FWR); collection Louis Carrier, Sainte-Anne de Bellevue, Que.; DIA purchase 14 February 1949.

BIBLIOGRAPHY
DIA, *French Canada,* p. 39, no. 149; Oglesby, fig. 158; DIA, *French in America,* pp. 199 (no. 532), 200 (ill.); Robinson, "Early Detroit," p. 6 (ill.); Fox, *Traditional Arts,* no. 40 (ill.).

EXHIBITIONS
Detroit 1946; Detroit 1951a; Detroit 1951b; Windsor 1953; Dearborn 1967; Windsor 1975

City Appropriation (acc. no. 49.22)

DESCRIPTION
Old English pattern: long, slender handle in a gentle arc expanding to rounded, turned-down end; hemispherical bowl and rounded double drop at back juncture of bowl and handle; front edge of handle outlined by narrow bright-cut band known as feather edge which simulates a gadrooned border; also bright-cut oval medallion with triple bud motif at upper end of handle.

143

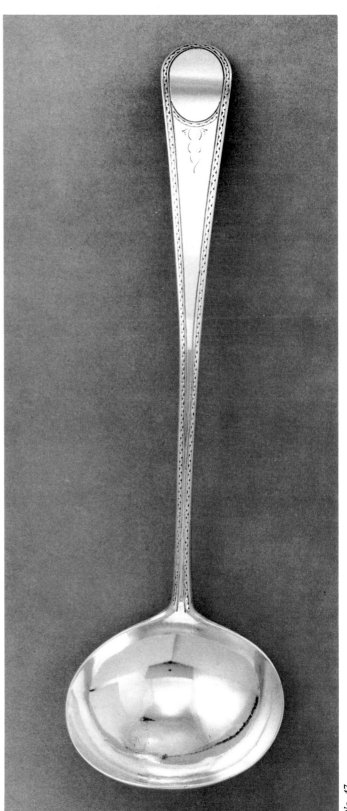

No. 47

In its restrained elegance and bright-cut engraving, this ladle is typical of the late eighteenth century. Schindler may have executed the engraving, or it may be the work of a specialized silversmith-engraver.

There were several engravers in Quebec City at this time. William Franckling was established there by 1779, and the partners Cummin and Douglas opened their shop in 1781, as did a recently arrived goldsmith from London, England, Thomas Powis (Langdon, *Canadian Silversmiths,* pp. 73, 62–63, 116). An even likelier possibility was Isaac Clements (also written Clemens and Clemence), a London-trained engraver and sometime silversmith. Clements arrived in Boston in 1774 and was an active Loyalist; he rented Paul Revere's shop in the winter of 1774–75. A testimony to Clements' expertise in engraving was his successful counterfeiting of American currency during the Revolution, two million pounds of which found its way into circulation. Clements was in Quebec City by 13 July 1780, when he advertised that "all Gentlemen may have Coats of Arms and Cyphers engraved on the shortest notice." By 1786, he was in Shelburne, Nova Scotia (Langdon, *American Silversmiths,* pp. 44–46).

While the provenance of this ladle is somewhat uncertain, it was made for the Bâby family and was found among Bâby descendants living in Lachine. Raymond Bâby (1688–1737) of Montreal had six sons, all of whom were possible owners. However, only two had any issue, Jacques Duperon (1731–1789), founder of the Detroit and Sandwich branch of the family, and François (1733–1820), founder of the Montreal branch. Whether either son had the ladle made cannot be determined, but one probably owned it eventually. Both brothers are known to have ordered silver from Schindler; moreover, both have descendants living in the Montreal-Lachine area. The problem of tracing the original owner is compounded by intermarriage between both family branches at a much later period.

There is a small silver cream jug by Schindler in the Henry Birks Collection (Q.124) which bears the inscription "Josephte Baby" and the heraldic crest of the Tarieu de Lanaudière family. Marie-Anne Tarieu de Lanaudière married François Bâby on 27 February 1786. The inscription probably refers to their daughter, Josephte-Thérèse, who was born in 1799, and thus was added to the jug some years after it was made. Schindler made other silver for the Bâby family, and in a letter addressed to François in 1778 by his brother and business partner Jacques Duperon, a Detroit fur trader, Schindler is mentioned as supplying them with Indian trade silver (Barbeau, "Indian Trade Silver," pp. 33–34).

Abbreviations

Archives

ANQM Archives Nationales du Québec, Montreal

ANQQ Archives Nationales du Québec, Quebec City

AQSG Archives Nationales du Québec, Section de Généalogie, Quebec City

BHC Burton Historical Collection, Detroit Public Library

CB Collection Bâby, Université de Montréal, Montreal

FMM Fort Malden Museum, Amherstburg, Ontario

FWR Francis W. Robinson files, Detroit Institute of Arts

IBC Inventaire des Biens Culturels, Quebec City [formerly Inventaire des Oeuvres d'Art du Québec]

RBMB Church Register of Baptisms, Marriages, and Burials

WLC William L. Clements Library, Ann Arbor, Michigan

Exhibitions

Dearborn 1964 "Arts and Crafts of the Old Northwest Territory." Greenfield Village and Henry Ford Museum, Dearborn, Michigan

Dearborn 1967 "Collecting Americana, Frontier Influences." Greenfield Village and Henry Ford Museum, Dearborn, Michigan

Detroit 1946 "The Arts of French Canada 1613–1870." Detroit Institute of Arts, Cleveland Museum of Art, Albany Institute of History and Art, Art Association of Montreal, National Gallery of Canada, Ottawa, and Musée de la Province de Québec [Musée du Québec], Quebec City

Detroit 1951a	"Folk Art Festival." Women's City Club, Detroit
Detroit 1951b	"The French in America 1520–1880." Detroit Institute of Arts
Grosse Pointe Woods 1973	"University Liggett Antiques Show." University Liggett School, Grosse Pointe Woods, Michigan
Grosse Pointe Woods 1975	"University Liggett Antiques Show." University Liggett School, Grosse Pointe Woods, Michigan
Ottawa 1974	"Silver in New France." National Gallery of Canada, Ottawa
Windsor 1953	"A Selection from the Louis Carrier Collection of Canadian Silver." Willistead Art Gallery [Art Gallery of Windsor]
Windsor 1975	"Traditional Arts of French Canada." Art Gallery of Windsor

Books and Articles

Allaire	Allaire, J.-B.-A. *Dictionnaire biographique du clergé canadien-français.* Vol. I: *Les anciens.* Montreal: n.p., 1910.
Barbeau, "Deux cents ans"	Barbeau, Marius. "Deux cents ans d'orfèvrerie chez nous." *Transactions of the Royal Society of Canada,* 3d ser., 33, sec. 1 (1939):183–91.
Barbeau, "Indian Trade Silver"	Barbeau, Marius. "Indian Trade Silver." *Transactions of the Royal Society of Canada,* 3d ser., 34, sec. 2 (1940):27–41.
Barbeau, *Trésor*	Barbeau, Marius. *Trésor des anciens Jésuites.* Série anthropologique, no. 43. Ottawa: National Museum of Canada, 1957.
BDIA	*Bulletin of the Detroit Institute of Arts*
Carré	Carré, Louis. *A Guide to Old French Plate.* 2d ed. London: Eyre and Spottiswoode, 1971.
Carrier	Carrier, Louis. "Silver of French Canada." Unpublished manuscript, FWR, 1946.
Casgrain	Casgrain, Philippe-Bâby. *Mémorial des familles Casgrain, Bâby et Perrault au Canada.* Quebec City: C. Darveau, 1898.
Cauchon and Juneau	Cauchon, Michel, and Juneau, André. "Landron, Jean-François." *Dictionary of Canadian Biography.* Vol. III: *1741 to 1770.* Toronto: University of Toronto Press, 1974.
Derome	Derome, Robert. *Les orfèvres de Nouvelle-France. Inventaire descriptif des sources.* Ottawa: National Gallery of Canada, 1974.
DIA, *French Canada*	*The Arts of French Canada 1613–1870.* Detroit: Detroit Institute of Arts, 1946.
DIA, *French in America*	*The French in America 1520–1880.* Detroit: Detroit Institute of Arts, 1951.
DIA, *Tannahill*	*The Robert Hudson Tannahill Gifts to the Detroit Institute of Arts.* Detroit: Detroit Institute of Arts, 1969.
Diderot	Diderot, Denis. *Encyclopédie, ou dictionnaire raisonné des sciences: Recueil de planches sur les sciences, les arts libéraux et les arts méchaniques avec leur explication.* Vol. VI. Paris: Briasson, 1772.
Doige	Doige, Thomas. *An Alphabetical List of the Merchants, Traders and Housekeepers, Residing in Montreal.* 1819. Reprint Montreal: Witness Printing House, 1899.
Fairbairn	Fairbairn, James, comp. *Fairbairn's Crests of the Families of Great Britain and Ireland.* Revised by Laurence Butters. Reprint Rutland, Vt.: Charles E. Tuttle, 1968.

Fox, "French Canadian Silver" — Fox, Ross. "French Canadian Silver." *University Liggett Antiques Show.* Grosse Pointe Woods, Mi., 1975. Pp. 76–81.

Fox, "Liturgical Silver" — Fox, Ross. "French Canadian Liturgical Silver." *BDIA* 52 (1973):97–105.

Fox, *Traditional Arts* — Fox, Ross. *Traditional Arts of French Canada.* Windsor, Ont.: Art Gallery of Windsor, 1975.

GQ — *La Gazette de Québec*

Grandjean — Grandjean, Serge. *L'orfèvrerie du XIXe siècle en Europe.* L'Oeil du Connaisseur. Paris: Presses Universitaires de France, 1962.

Greening — Greening, W. E. "Silversmiths of French Canada." *Connoisseur* 162 (1966):213–17.

Helft — Helft, Jacques. *Les grands orfèvres de Louis XIII à Charles X.* Collection Grands Artisans d'Autrefois. Paris: Hachette, 1965.

Ignatieff — Ignatieff, Helena. "Silver." In *The Book of Canadian Antiques,* edited by Donald Blake Webster. Toronto: McGraw-Hill Ryerson, 1974.

Langdon, *American Silversmiths* — Langdon, John E. *American Silversmiths in British North America 1776–1800.* Toronto: n.p., 1970.

Langdon, "Canadian Silver" — Langdon, John E. *Canadian Silversmiths 1700–1900.* Stinehour, 1966.

Langdon, *Canadian Silversmiths* — Langdon, John E. *Canadian Silversmiths 1700–1900.* Toronto: Stinehour, 1966.

Langdon, *Marks* — Langdon, John E. *Guide to Marks on Early Canadian Silver: Eighteenth and Nineteenth Centuries.* 2d ed. Toronto: Ryerson, 1969.

Magnan — Magnan, Hormisdas. *Dictionnaire historique et géographique des paroisses, missions et municipalités de la province de Québec.* Arthabaska, Que.: Imprimerie d'Arthabaska, 1925.

Massicotte — Massicotte, É.-Z. "L'argentier Huguet-Latour." *Bulletin des Recherches Historiques* 46 (1940):284–87.

Massicotte and Roy — Massicotte, É.-Z., and Roy, Régis. *Armorial du Canada français.* Montreal: Beauchemin, 1915.

Maurault — Maurault, Olivier. "Les trésors d'une église de campagne." *Transactions of the Royal Society of Canada,* 3d ser., 41, sec. 1 (1947):54–62.

Métis — *Un siècle de labeur de roi d'honneur—histoire de la paroisse de Saint-Octave de Métis, 1855–1955.* Matane, Que.: Comité des Recherches Historiques de Saint-Octave de Métis, 1955.

Meyers and Hanlan — Meyers, R. M., and Hanlan, J. F. "The Compositional Analysis of French-Canadian Church Silver." *Bulletin of the National Gallery of Canada, Ottawa* 21 (1973):22–33.

Morisset, *Cap-Santé* — Morisset, Gérard. *Le Cap-Santé: Ses églises et son trésor.* Collection Champlain. Quebec City: Médium, 1944.

Morisset, *Évolution* — Morisset, Gérard. *Évolution d'une pièce d'argenterie.* Collection Champlain. Quebec City: n.p., 1943

Morisset, *Lambert* — Morisset, Gérard. *Paul Lambert dit Saint-Paul.* Collection Champlain. Quebec City: Médium, 1945.

Morisset, "L'instrument" — Morisset, Gérard. "L'instrument de paix." *Transactions of the Royal Society of Canada,* 3d ser., 39, sec. 1 (1945):143–52.

Morisset, "L'orfèvre Lambert"	Morisset, Gérard. "L'orfèvre Paul Lambert dit Saint-Paul." *La Patrie* [Montreal], 1 January 1950, pp. 14, 38.
Morisset, "L'orfèvrerie canadienne"	Morisset, Gérard. "L'orfèvrerie canadienne." *Technique* [Montreal] 22 (1947):83–88.
Morisset, "L'orfèvrerie française"	Morisset, Gérard. "L'orfèvrerie française au Canada." *La Patrie* [Montreal], 22 October 1950, pp. 26–27, 55.
Morisset, *Lotbinière*	Morisset, Gérard. *Les églises et le trésor de Lotbinière.* Collection Champlain. Quebec City: Charrier et Dugal, 1953.
Morisset, "Morand"	Morisset, Gérard. "L'orfèvre Paul Morand, 1784–1854." *Transactions of the Royal Society of Canada,* 3d ser., 48, sec. 1 (1954):29–35.
Morisset, "Paradis"	Morisset, Gérard. "L'orfèvre Roland Paradis." *La Patrie* [Montreal], 26 November 1950, pp. 26, 31.
Morisset, "Un perruquier-orfèvre"	Morisset, Gérard. "Un perruquier-orfèvre." *La Patrie* [Montreal], 2 July 1950, pp. 28–29, 31.
Morisset, "Roland Paradis"	Morisset, Gérard. "L'orfèvre Roland Paradis." *Technique* [Montreal] 29 (1954):437–42.
Morisset, "Saint-Martin"	Morisset, Gérard. "Saint-Martin (Ile-Jésus) après le sinistre 19 du mai." *Technique* [Montreal] 17 (1942): 597–605.
Morisset, "Saint-Pierre"	Morisset, Gérard. "L'église de Saint-Pierre de Montmagny." *La Patrie* [Montreal], 3 December 1950, pp. 26–27, 50.
Morisset, "Sasseville"	Morisset, Gérard. "L'orfèvre François Sasseville." *Transactions of the Royal Society of Canada,* 3d ser., 49, sec. 1 (1955):51–54.
Morisset, "Sculpture"	Morisset, Gérard. "Sculpture et arts décoratifs." *Vie des Arts,* no. 26 (1962):38–42.
Morisset, *Varennes*	Morisset, Gérard. *Les églises et le trésor de Varennes.* Collection Champlain. Quebec City: Médium, 1943.
Morisset, "XVIIIe siècle"	Morisset, Gérard. "Notre orfèvrerie au XVIIIe siècle." *Forces* [Montreal], no. 5 (1968):14–19.
Oglesby	Oglesby, Catharine. *French Provincial Decorative Art.* New York: Scribner's, 1951.
Paradis and Morisset	Paradis, Alexandre, and Morisset, Gérard. *Kamouraska (1674–1948).* Quebec City: n.p., 1948.
Ranvoyzé	*François Ranvoyzé orfèvre 1739–1819.* Quebec City: Musée du Québec, 1968.
Raymond	Raymond, Percy E. "Crown-Handled Porringers." *Pewter Collectors' Club* 111 (1958):144–49.
Remembrancer	*The Remembrancer: or, Impartial Repository of Public Events, For the Year 1778.* Vol. VI. London: J. Almon, 1778.
Robinson, "Detroit Silversmith"	Robinson, Francis W. "New Light on an Early Detroit Silversmith." *BDIA* 40 (1960–61):22–23.
Robinson, "Early Detroit"	Robinson, Francis W. "Silversmiths of Early Detroit." *Bulletin of the Detroit Historical Society* 9 (1952):5–8.
Robinson, "Indian Trade Silver"	Robinson, Francis W. "Notes on Indian Trade Silver in the Collection of Mr. Lamont Jones, Waterville, Ohio." *Ohio Archaeologist* 7 (1957):9–16.
Roy, *De Tonnancour*	Roy, Pierre-Georges. *La famille Godefroy de Tonnancour.* Lévis, Que.: LaFlamme, 1904.
Roy, "Hubert"	Roy, Pierre-Georges. "La famille Hubert." *Bulletin des Recherches Historiques* 40 (1934):756–61.
Simmons	Simmons, Walter E. "The Collector Looks at Detroit Silver." *University Liggett Antiques Show.* Grosse Pointe Woods, Mi., 1973. Pp. 21–26.

Tanguay

Tanguay, Cyprien. *Dictionnaire généalogique des familles canadiennes depuis la fondation de la colonie jusqu'à nos jours.* 7 vols. Montreal: Eusèbe Sénécal, 1871–90.

Tardy

Les poinçons de garantie internationaux pour l'argent. 11th ed. Paris: Tardy, 1975.

Traquair

Traquair, Ramsay. *The Old Silver of Quebec.* Toronto: Macmillan, 1940.

Trudel

Trudel, Jean. *Silver in New France.* Ottawa: National Gallery of Canada, 1974.

Appendix I

Silver Inventories

The types and quantities of silver owned by colonists and churches is best elucidated through a study of inventories. While an in-depth analysis of inventories is beyond the scope of this catalogue, a few of them, representative of the more important patrons of Quebec silversmiths, are cited below.

Throughout the late eighteenth and nineteenth centuries, the bourgeoisie was the mainstay of the domestic trade. An indication of the silver owned by persons of this class is found in three inventories of the Guy family of Montreal. Dating from the eighteenth and early nineteenth centuries, they range over the most important periods of silver production in Quebec.

When Elizabeth Garreau, first wife of the Montreal merchant Pierre-Théodore Guy, died in June 1734, their possessions included twelve spoons, twelve forks, one coffee spoon, one soup ladle, one stew spoon, one écuelle, one plate, two chafing dishes, two salts, and five tumblers. Totaling 124 ounces, this silver was valued at 798 livres, 5 sols.[1] There is no indication as to whether this silver was imported or made in the colony; probably it was a mixture. An inventory drawn up on 1 December 1770, after the death of Marianne Truillier, second wife of Pierre-Théodore Guy, reveals an increase in the family silver: one soup tureen, one large oval plate, four shaped plates, two shaped bowls, one écuelle, one water ewer, one pair of candlesticks, one pair of snuffers and tray, one olive spoon, one tumbler, six spoons and forks with threaded edge, six plain spoons and forks. Totaling 440 ounces, this silver was valued at 2,970 livres.[2] The plates and bowls with a shaped edge and the flatware with a threaded edge were undoubtedly of French origin, as these designs were not in use by Quebec silversmiths at this time.

The inventory, drawn up on 15 September 1813, of the household goods of Étienne Guy, a surveyor and lieutenant-colonel of the militia in Montreal and a grandson of Pierre-Théodore, contained two candlesticks, two bowls, two plates, one pair of snuffers and tray, two ewers, one coffee pot, four salts, twelve small spoons, eleven soup spoons, one large spoon, one pair of sugar tongs, and one sauceboat with spoon. Totaling 283 ounces, 4 gros, it was valued at 70 louis, 15 shillings.[3] Most if not all of this silver was probably made by Quebec silversmiths. An unusual absence in this inventory is a teapot, which most bourgeois families certainly owned in this period. As indicated in the above inventories, silver was probably not any more common in bourgeois households of the early nineteenth century than it was in the mid-eighteenth century.

By the end of the eighteenth century, most churches were well supplied with silver vessels, even modest rural ones such as Saint-Michel de Vaudreuil, near Montreal. The following inventory from that church was recorded in 1809 (all vessels were acquired after 1775 and thus can be assumed to be the work of Quebec silversmiths): one monstrance, two chalices with patens, one sanctuary lamp, one censer with incense-boat, two pairs of cruets with trays, one cup for purifications, one ciborium, one porte-dieu (pyx), one chrismatory with three ampullae, and one processional cross.[4]

NOTES TO APPENDIX I

1. CB, A6, Montréal, 30 June 1734, box. 20.

2. CB, A5, Montréal, 1 December 1770, box 13.

3. ANQM, Louis Huguet-Latour minutes, 15 September 1813.

4. E.-R. Adair, "The Church of Saint-Michel de Vaudreuil," *Bulletin des Recherches Historiques* 49 (1943):82–86.

Appendix II

Elemental Analysis

The elemental composition of pieces in the Detroit collection was analyzed by means of energy-dispersive X-ray fluorescence spectroscopy at the Henry Francis du Pont Winterthur Museum. These analyses were conducted by Janice Carlson and Karen Papouchado, under the direction of Victor F. Hanson, in July and December 1974.[1] All catalogue entries were analyzed except Nos. 13, 15, 18, 22, 23, 29, 42, and 46, which were not available for analysis, and two additional pieces, an ornament in the shape of a beaver (DIA acc. no. 73.198) by Robert Cruickshank and a plate (DIA acc. no. 72.223) attributed to Jean-François Landron. The Cruickshank ornament has not been catalogued because of its relative insignificance and the Landron plate because it is not authentic.

The primary purpose of this type of analysis is the authentication of pieces by detecting trace elements which are normally present in older pieces but are absent in modern repairs, replacements, or outright forgeries. Fourteen elements were measured and listed in the accompanying table.[2] Interpretation of the analytical results is limited by the relatively small number of pieces involved and their great span in time, from about 1719 until the late nineteenth century. The present conclusions have been greatly augmented by the data and interpretations resulting from a similar study conducted recently by R. M. Meyers and J. F. Hanlan of the Canadian Conservation Institute at Ottawa.[3] The Ottawa study dealt with 32 pieces of ecclesiastical silver at the National Gallery of Canada, two-thirds of which were by three major silversmiths of the period from 1760 to 1867. Meyers and Hanlan were able to discern some general trends in the metallic composition of Quebec ecclesiastical silver during that period, trends which are largely corroborated by the present study, but some variant readings were also obtained which suggest that they are not as fixed as one might hope. The elemental analysis of the Detroit pieces also adds a new, if somewhat limited, insight into the composition of Quebec domestic silver. The French pieces are not included in the following discussion, as they are too few and of uncertain provenance.

During the French regime in Canada, before 1759, domestic silver appears to have had a silver content at or slightly below the Paris standard of 95.83 percent.[4] The Detroit pieces in this category have silver readings between 93.6 and 95.5 percent (Nos. 6, 30, and 35). As native silver was not available in Canada before about 1870, early eighteenth-century silversmiths derived their material from worn-out French plate and coin—French, English, Portuguese, and Spanish. It is not known whether plate or coin was the more important source.[5] The metallic composition of the three Detroit pieces reflects a dependence on old plate with a possible addition of small amounts of coin. If coin alone were used, there would have been a more significant drop from the Paris standard in the silver percentage, as the standard of silver coinage at the time was about 90 percent.[6]

The only ecclesiastical piece from this period for which readings could be obtained, a cruet (No. 5), has an average silver reading similar to the above, at 93.84 percent.[7] The provenance of this piece is uncertain; moreover, if it is Canadian, it may be aberrant. Stylistically it is unusual. The Ottawa study clearly indicates that in the late eighteenth century most ecclesiastical silver had a silver content above 95 percent, often as high as 97 percent,[8] largely because of the practice of fashioning new church pieces from old and the desire of silversmiths to use only high purity silver for sacred vessels. Certainly there must have been an even greater dependence on remelted French plate in the first half of the century and, in consequence, a silver content at about the Paris standard.

The Detroit collection has a large number of church pieces which date from the first half of the nineteenth century. When their readings are coupled with the Ottawa data, more precise conclusions about the composition of church silver during that period can be drawn. Generally the silver content of church vessels declined, and most range between 93 and 95 percent, between the Paris and the sterling standards. This decline occurred earlier and is more pronounced in Montreal than in Quebec City. There are four fully authenticated pieces at Detroit by two Montreal silversmiths, dated between 1800 and 1854.[9] When the silver readings of each piece are averaged, two fall within a 93- to 95-percent range (Nos. 25 and 32), the others between 91.5 and 93 percent (Nos. 26 and 33). All church silver of the same period by Montreal silversmiths which was analyzed at Ottawa is in the first category, including a holy water stoup by Huguet, a pax by Polonceau, a ciborium by Cruickshank, a pax by Morand, and a ciborium by Salomon Marion.[10]

The pieces by Laurent Amiot of Quebec City, all dating between about 1800 and 1839, have a slightly higher silver content. Three Amiot pieces at Detroit (Nos. 8, 11, and 12) and three at Ottawa are above 95 percent; three at Detroit (Nos. 7, 9, and 10) and four at Ottawa are between 93 and 95 percent; and one at Ottawa is between 91.5 and 93 percent. By mid-century and after, the silver content of Quebec church silver approaches that of Montreal. Two pieces by Sasseville at Detroit are above 95 percent (Nos. 43 and 44);[11] four Ottawa pieces are between 93 and 95 percent; two Ottawa pieces are below 93 percent. Thus there is a general downward trend in silver purity from the eighteenth century until the fourth quarter of the nineteenth century. This downward trend occurred first in Montreal and was not significant in Quebec City until the 1840s, and it was not absolutely consistent: frequent exceptions are noted. For example, the two Detroit ciboria by Sasseville are at or above the level of 95 percent silver. In spite of these exceptions, a definite diminution in silver purity did occur and is seen in the late nineteenth-century reliquary cross (No. 24) by Robert Hendery, which has a reading of 88.05 percent.

The silver used for the church plate made in Quebec City was of a higher purity than that of Montreal in the first half of the nineteenth century possibly because old French plate was more readily available in Quebec City and its environs. In the early eighteenth century, the Quebec City area was more populous than Montreal; in the next century the position was reversed. Quebec City must have received more early imported French silver than Montreal; in the nineteenth century Quebec City silversmiths had access to more old French plate, while the demands of the market were less than those of Montreal. Thus French plate continued to be melted down for church vessels, and English plate and coin were also increasingly relied on, especially at Montreal. The silver readings of the Montreal pieces, generally averaging 93 or 94 percent are very similar to those of English plate of the last half of the eighteenth and the first half of the nineteenth centuries.[12] Amiot and Sasseville also must have used English plate, as the majority of their pieces are within the same range.

By the late eighteenth century coin appears to have been widely used as the material for domestic silver. This is particularly evident in the flatware readings, which also suggest that in some instances small amounts of copper were added to the melt. Generally, during the early nineteenth century domestic pieces are at or below the sterling standard and thus slightly below the silver purity level of church pieces. Flatware is often lower than holloware and is within the standard of American coin silver at 89.2 percent.

Measurement of the gold content is also very illuminating. Church silver usually has a much higher gold count than British or American silver and is higher than most Quebec domestic and trade silver.[13] The church pieces (excluding parts known to have been replaced) range from 0.02 to 0.92 percent gold but are usually between 0.2 and 0.5 percent. The high gold content tends to reaffirm the idea that silversmiths depended on old French church vessels as raw material for new ones; such vessels were often partially gilt, and when melted down the gold would become incorporated into the new melt, creating a higher gold trace than that found in domestic silver. Gold percentages in domestic silver vary from 0 to 0.53 percent but usually fall in the range from 0.08 to about 0.3 percent, and the four pieces of Indian trade silver average about 0.1 percent.

The mercury readings reveal the method of gilding, mercury (amalgam) or electrodeposition. Readings were taken of the gilt parts of nine pieces (Nos. 1, 7, 11, 16, 25, 31, 33, 43, and 44): five were mercury-gilt, four electrogilt.[14] The mercury-gilt pieces all date before 1840, as would be expected: all gilding was done by the process of mercury- or fire-gilding until the nineteenth century. Isolated examples of electro-gilding are known in England and France in the early nineteenth century, and it became widespread after 1840.[15] One of the first recorded instances of its use in Quebec was in 1858. That year Pierre Lespérance, François Sasseville's partner, electro-gilded a monstrance which Sasseville had made for Notre-Dame Basilica in Quebec City.[16] Both Detroit ciboria by Sasseville were also gilded by this method. One piece (No. 43) is known to date from 1852, suggesting an even earlier date for the introduction of electro-gilding into Quebec.

The two other electro-gilt pieces at Detroit are of an earlier date, however. The Morand ciborium (No. 33) could have been regilt by electrolysis in the present century, or the gilding could date from the last years of Morand's career. While he is not known to have used this technique, he died in 1854, two years after the evidence suggests that it was used by Sasseville. Could Morand have been familiar with this new technique as well? The other deviant piece is a ciborium by Robert Cruickshank and Guillaume Loir (No. 16). Large areas of this piece may also be silverplated, and therefore the electro-gilding is not such an anomaly. Both silverplating and electro-gilding were probably added at the same time during this century. Modern electroplating of old vessels is not at all unusual, and Meyers and Hanlan discovered three such examples.[17]

Analyses of silver and gold content provide an invaluable guide in determining the authenticity of a piece of silver. An individual piece usually has a spread of not more than 2 percent in the silver readings of the various components. If the spread is 4 percent or greater, there is an obvious reason to suspect that the portion with the deviant reading has been replaced or repaired. Replacement can often be confirmed by stylistic analysis. For example, the cups of chalices were sometimes replaced, and late examples usually had a more pronounced flare to the lip and a rounder bottom, like No. 2 (see also Nos. 17 and 31). The gold content is also revealing because refining techniques were greatly improved in the nineteenth century, and a purer silver resulted. The first advances were made in France in the 1820s, when chemical methods were developed to extract much finer amounts of gold and some other trace elements. These new techniques were soon adopted in England.[18] The most significant improvement occurred in the late nineteenth century, the introduction of electrolytic refining. The Moebius process, patented in 1884, was one of the more successful of the early techniques. With it silver of 99.9 percent purity could be obtained.[19] Electrolytic refining came into general use by the turn of the twentieth century and probably began to be used in Canada at about this time.[20]

Gold and other trace elements such as lead and zinc, which are naturally found together, were now effectively removed from silver. Thus silver-gold ratios can serve as a relative indicator of age; if gold is present, of course, we know that the object is over a hundred years old.[21] While the products of refining methods exhibit characteristics which may be used to date silver, remelted older silver may be used at a later date, so that correct composition is no proof of the authenticity of a piece. For example, an early twentieth-century piece could have a high gold count. The reverse also occurs occasionally: we may find an early nineteenth-century piece with a low gold count. There are three such in the Detroit collection, a fork (No. 45) by

Sasseville at 0.05 percent, an incense-boat (No. 27) by Huguet at 0.04 percent and a snuffbox (No. 34) by Morand at 0 percent.[22]

Geometry can also be a factor in these readings:[23] if during measurement the object did not fit exactly over the ring-shaped radiation source, the accuracy of the readings could be affected. This problem is particularly troublesome in the case of small objects and those with an irregular surface, such as the fork and incense-boat. Other factors should also be considered, including the possible use of polishes containing high-purity silver but no gold, or silverplating. Native silver is occasionally found with a negligible gold trace.[24] However, a more plausible explanation lies in the improved French and English silver-refining techniques of the 1820s.[25] Sasseville and Morand could very well have had access to the new improved English coin. However, Huguet died in 1829, and it is highly unlikely that he used such coin. This raises the question whether the Huguet incense-boat is in fact French and whether it was made in the 1830s or later.

If a piece lacks a gold trace and has only minute amounts of base metals, except for copper, if the style and mark are questionable and the provenance unknown, it is undoubtedly a forgery. A case in point is a scalloped plate at Detroit formerly attributed to Jean-François Landron (72.223) which has a molded rim and engraved monogram typical of the nineteenth century and a highly suspect mark (fig. 4). This piece conforms to the nineteenth-century French silver standard of 95 percent and is probably French and made later in that century.

Elemental analysis of an individual piece can provide valuable information in authenticating parts or the whole. Regarding the overall compositional spectrum of Quebec silver, precise conclusions about particular periods or silversmiths are wanting, and at present the analytical results can only supply some very general outlines. There is a great variation in the elemental composition of Quebec silver in all periods. It is at present apparent that elemental analysis alone cannot distinguish a piece made in Quebec, for example, from a French or English piece, whereas Victor Hanson reports that the readings of English and American silver exhibit a more definite pattern and can be distinguished with a high degree of accuracy solely on the basis of metallic content.[26]

NOTES TO APPENDIX II

1. Known as Project 272, the report, "Results of French Canadian Silver Analysis," was written by Janice Carlson and Karen Papouchado. It is hereafter referred to as the Winterthur study. For a description of the analytical technique employed, see Victor F. Hanson, "Quantitative Elemental Analysis of Art Objects by Energy-Dispersive X-ray Fluorescence Spectroscopy," *Applied Spectroscopy* 27 (1973):309–33.

2. The data in the table are extracted from the Winterthur study and are rearranged in the order of the entries in this catalogue.

3. "The Compositional Analysis of French-Canadian Church Silver," *Bulletin of the National Gallery of Canada, Ottawa* 21 (1973):22–33. It is hereafter referred to as the Ottawa study.

4. Louis Carré, *A Guide to Old French Plate*, 2d ed. (London: Eyre and Spottiswoode, 1971), p. 6.

5. Early archival records contain numerous references to the melting of coin and old plate, but the supply of both was inadequate. The shortage of coinage as currency was alleviated by the extensive use of paper or card money in the colony (Marcel Trudel, *Initiation à la Nouvelle-France*, 2d ed. [Montreal: Holt, Rinehart and Winston, 1971], pp. 198–200). The general deficiency in raw material undoubtedly explains why so many of the larger and more important silver commissions of the gentry and churches were sent to France.

6. This standard was generally followed from 1726 to 1793, when 90 percent became strictly enforced. The composition of earlier silver coin cannot be determined without extensive analyses, as coinage was frequently debased; however, the silver content was probably below 90 percent (Marc Bloch, *Esquisse d'une histoire monétaire de l'Europe*, Cahiers des Annales [Paris: Armand Colin, 1954], pp. 79–80). English coin adhered to the sterling standard of 92.5 percent from 1560 until 1920 (Gerald Taylor, *Silver*, 2d ed. [Harmondsworth: Penguin Books, 1969], p. 161). The standard for Spanish silver coin was 93.05 percent from 1535 to 1728 and 91.66 percent thereafter (Lawrence Anderson, *The Art of the Silversmith in Mexico 1519–1936* [New York: Oxford University Press, 1941], I, 117–19). The Portuguese standard was 90.6 percent (John Craig, *The Mint: A History of the London Mint from A.D. 287 to 1948* [Cambridge: Cambridge University Press, 1953], pp. 375, 391). Silver coin in the United States followed the sterling standard until 1792, when the silver content was lowered to 89.2 percent. In 1837 this standard was raised to 90 percent (Martha Gandy Fales, *Early American Silver*, 2d ed. [New York: E. P. Dutton, 1973], p. 232). These standards were adhered to within reasonable limits; that is, coin at any given period probably did not deviate much more than 1 percent from the established standard. This is especially true of English coin. Assay methods in that country were highly developed: assay by touchstone was accurate within 1 or 2 percent; assay by cupellation was 0.3 to 0.5 percent accurate. However, other allowances have to be made. For example, the trial plate used by the London mint from 1728 until 1828 had a purity silver which was 0.4 percent too fine at 92.89 percent. This plate was the standard of reference for all coin and plate produced in Great Britain during that period (Craig, *The Mint*, pp. 23, 74, 307–8, 337).

7. The ciborium by Landron (No. 31) is not included here, as it may be partially silverplated.

8. Ottawa study, p. 28.

9. The incense-boat by Huguet (No. 27) is not included because it had some unusual readings, which raise some questions about its provenance. Three other pieces have also been excluded: the Cruickshank chalice (No. 17), as only the foot is original; the Loir and Cruickshank ciborium (No. 16), as it may be partially silverplated (see p. 58); and the stoup by "HP" (No. 38), as it is of uncertain date.

10. Ottawa study, pp. 26–27.

11. *Ibid.*, p. 26. The Detroit ciborium (No. 44) is silver-gilt, but if the gold content is set aside and the data recalculated, the silver content is about 95 percent (Winterthur study, p. 1).

12. Victor F. Hanson, "The Curator's Dream Instrument," Paper Presented at the Symposium "Applications of Science in the Examination of Works of Art," Boston Museum of Fine Arts, June 1970, pp. 28–29; see also Hanson, "Elemental Analysis," p. 329.

13. Winterthur study, p. 3.

14. Communication of Victor H. Hanson, 22 April 1975.

15. Electro-gilding did not entirely replace the older method of mercury-gilding, which continued to be used in Canada during the early twentieth century.

16. Gérard Morisset, "L'orfèvre François Sasseville," *Transactions of the Royal Society of Canada*, 3d ser., 49, sec. 1 (1955):52–53.

17. Ottawa study, pp. 26–27.

18. Craig, *The Mint,* pp. 304–5; F. W. Gibbs, ''Extractions and Production of Metals: Non-Ferrous Metals,'' in *A History of Technology,* IV: *The Industrial Revolution c. 1750 to c. 1850,* ed. Charles Singer et al., 4th ed. (Oxford: Clarendon Press, 1970), pp. 142–43.

19. Electrolytic refining was introduced in Wales as early as 1869 (R. Chadwick, ''New Extraction Processes for Metals,'' in *ibid.,* V: *The Late 19th Century c. 1850 to c. 1900,* pp. 96–97; see also Taylor, *Silver,* p. 49.

20. Silver was not mined in Canada in any quantity until the 1870s, with the opening of operations at the Silver Islet mine on Lake Superior in 1872. By the end of the century that country was among the four leading silver producers in the world. Thus Canada would have been most receptive to the new refining technology (John Percy, *Silver and Gold—Part I, Metallurgy: The Art of Extracting Metals from Their Ores* [London: John Murray, 1880], pp. 191–96, 517; Harold A. Innis, ''Settlement and the Mining Frontier,'' in *Canadian Frontiers of Settlement,* ed. W. A. Mackintosh and W. L. G. Joerg, IX [Toronto: MacMillan of Canada, 1936], pp. 272–76, 286; Y. S. Loeng, *Silver: An Analysis of Factors Affecting Its Price* [Washington, D.C.: Brookings Institution, 1934], pp. 58–59).

21. There is no absolute cutoff point after which a sudden reduction occurs in the gold count of all silver plate. In most but not all cases, if the gold is about 0.05 percent or less, the piece was probably made after the middle of the nineteenth century (communication of Janice H. Carlson, 19 May 1975). It should also be noted that forgers can adjust the levels of gold and silver to reproduce compositional percentages associated with particular periods. The forging of Canadian silver has not yet reached such a level of sophistication, but this problem no doubt will have to be reckoned with in the future.

22. The French chalice (No. 2) also has low gold readings for the foot and stem. These parts are unquestionably dated in the late seventeenth century, but the cup, with no gold count, is dated twentieth century.

23. According to Ralph T. Overman and Herbert M. Clark, one of many possible sources of error in radioactivity measurements is a ''variation in radiation intensity reaching the detector due to uncertainties in positioning radioactive sources relative to the detector'' (*Radioisotope Techniques* [New York: McGraw-Hill, 1960], p. 99).

24. The analysis of Umayyad silver coins from northwestern Iran (ca. A.D. 661–749) shows gold traces ranging below 0.2 percent and as low as 0.01 percent (Darcy G. Shepherd, ''An Art Historian Looks at the Gordus Report,'' Paper presented at the ''Sasanian Colloquies,'' Metropolitan Museum of Art, New York, January 1973, p. 9.

25. Cf. the readings for late nineteenth-century English silver in Hanson, ''The Curator's Dream Instrument,'' p. 29.

26. Hanson, ''Elemental Analysis,'' pp. 327, 329.

Elemental Analysis of Catalogue Entries

Entry	Ag	Mn	Fe	Co	Ni	Cu	As	Pb	Zn	Au	Hg	Cd	Sn	Sb
1. Ciborium (69.13)														
cover	95.65	0	.02	0	.02	3.45	.02	.38	.09	.30	.03	0	.02	0
bowl (outside)	94.66	0	.03	.03	.01	4.50	0	.35	.06	.28	.06	0	.01	0
bowl (inside, gilt)	54.08	.07	.14	.23	.16	3.71	.42	1.22	.55	30.30	9.02	0	.05	.06
calyx	96.43	0	.02	0	0	2.75	.01	.32	.08	.32	.04	0	.02	0
knop	97.47	0	0	0	0	1.71	.01	.30	.09	.36	.04	0	.01	0
foot	95.39	0	.04	.01	.02	3.88	0	.31	.04	.26	.03	0	.01	0
2. Chalice (69.172)														
cup (outside)	92.57	0	.02	.02	.02	7.30	0	0	.03	0	0	0	.01	0
knop	97.15	0	.02	0	0	2.46	0	.27	.01	.06	.01	0	.01	0
foot	96.44	0	.01	0	.01	3.19	.02	.22	.02	.08	.01	0	0	0
3. Plate (71.34)														
obverse (near engraving)	94.87	0	.01	.05	.02	4.24	0	.48	.02	.30	0	0	0	0
reverse (repair to rim)	99.31	0	.01	0	0	.45	0	.11	0	.08	0	0	.03	0
4. Plate (70.561)														
obverse (near engraving)	97.14	0	0	.01	.03	2.45	0	.15	.01	.19	0	0	.01	0
obverse (opposite engraving)	97.52	0	.01	.04	.02	2.02	0	.15	.01	.18	0	.02	.03	0
reverse	98.09	0	0	0	.01	1.54	0	.12	0	.17	.01	0	.04	0
reverse (after sanding)	97.58	0	.01	.02	.01	1.94	0	.16	.01	.16	0	0	.08	0

Chemical Symbols: Ag, silver; Mn, manganese; Fe, iron; Co, cobalt; Ni, nickel; Cu, copper; As, arsenic; Pb, lead; Zn, zinc; Au, gold; Hg, mercury; Cd, cadmium; Sn, tin; Sb, antimony.

Note: Nos. 13, 15, 18, 22, 23, 29, 42, and 46 were not available for analysis.

Entry	Ag	Mn	Fe	Co	Ni	Cu	As	Pb	Zn	Au	Hg	Cd	Sn	Sb
5. Cruet (69.265)														
body	93.82	.01	.02	.04	.02	5.03	0	.44	.09	.44	.05	0	0	.03
lid	93.86	.01	.01	.01	.02	5.30	0	.26	.15	.32	.03	0	.01	0
6. Écuelle (57.220)														
bottom	93.94	.02	.02	.02	.03	4.99	0	.29	.10	.53	.04	0	.03	0
left handle (reverse)	95.50	.01	.01	0	.02	3.73	.01	.25	.11	.28	.02	0	.02	.04
right handle (reverse)	93.90	0	.02	.02	.02	5.23	0	.33	.14	.28	.02	0	.02	0
7. Ciborium (69.297)														
cover	94.18	0	.02	.02	.02	5.22	.01	.17	.03	.30	.02	0	.01	0
bowl (outside)	94.81	0	.02	.02	.01	4.56	0	.21	.03	.28	.06	0	0	0
bowl (inside, gilt)	79.08	.02	.07	.08	.06	4.98	.10	.30	.26	12.18	2.79	0	.06	0
calyx	93.84	0	.01	.03	.02	5.62	0	.15	.03	.26	.03	0	0	0
knop	94.16	0	.02	0	.01	5.22	0	.21	.03	.31	.03	0	0	0
foot	93.94	0	.01	.02	.02	5.42	0	.21	.04	.29	.04	0	.01	0
8. Censer (57.145)														
bowl	97.30	.01	0	.01	.02	2.21	0	.19	.03	.18	.02	0	.02	0
spur	96.91	.01	.03	0	.01	2.69	0	.19	.04	.08	.01	0	.01	0
9. Cruet (53.320a)														
body	94.41	0	0	.02	.02	4.55	0	.36	.05	.52	.04	0	.01	0
Cruet (53.320b)														
body	94.17	.01	.01	.02	.02	4.83	0	.35	.06	.50	.04	0	0	0
Tray (53.320c)														
obverse	93.37	.01	.02	.04	.03	5.93	0	.24	.09	.21	.02	0	.03	0
reverse	93.52	.01	0	.01	.01	5.67	0	.39	.10	.24	.02	0	.01	0
10. Censer (71.33)														
bowl	94.72	0	.02	0	.01	4.57	.02	.42	.05	.15	.02	0	0	0
spur	93.72	0	.02	0	.01	5.61	0	.15	.04	.37	.04	0	.03	0
foot	94.64	0	.02	0	.02	4.75	0	.22	.04	.26	.03	0	.01	0
chain	93.29	0	.05	.03	.02	5.92	.02	.15	.10	.33	.04	.01	.03	0
finger-plate	94.83	0	.04	.02	.02	4.54	.01	.24	.04	.21	.03	0	.02	0

Entry	Ag	Mn	Fe	Co	Ni	Cu	As	Pb	Zn	Au	Hg	Cd	Sn	Sb
11. Chalice (70.834)														
cup (inside, gilt)	64.26	.04	.08	.16	.11	3.03	.26	.61	.46	24.96	5.95	0	.06	.01
calyx	95.50	0	.02	.03	.01	3.86	0	.23	.04	.26	.02	0	.02	0
knop	95.22	.01	.02	.02	.01	4.17	0	.20	.05	.26	.02	0	.01	0
12. Incense-boat (68.161)														
lid (front)	95.23	0	.02	0	.01	4.18	.01	.12	.05	.33	.04	0	0	0
lid (back)	95.87	0	.01	0	.02	3.56	0	.12	.04	.32	.04	0	.02	0
boat	95.08	0	.02	0	.01	4.25	0	.14	.06	.38	.04	0	.02	0
14. Tablespoon (64.85)														
bowl (reverse)	90.67	.01	.03	.02	.03	8.76	0	.22	.07	.15	.01	0	.02	0
handle (obverse)	91.59	.01	.03	.03	.02	7.86	0	.22	.06	.14	.01	0	.02	0
16. Ciborium (72.467)														
cover	98.81	0	.01	0	.01	.91	0	.11	.01	.11	.01	0	.01	0
bowl (outside)	95.50	0	.01	.01	.02	4.10	.02	.17	.02	.14	.02	0	0	0
bowl (inside, gilt)	90.18	.01	.04	.04	.03	3.11	.06	.14	.11	5.65	.56	0	.06	0
knop	99.00	0	0	0	0	.85	.01	.06	.01	.06	0	0	0	0
foot	98.02	0	.01	0	0	1.79	.02	.09	.01	.04	.01	0	0	0
17. Chalice (69.171)														
cup (outside)	92.68	0	.02	0	.02	7.22	0	0	.04	0	0	0	0	0
knop	92.93	0	.02	0	.02	6.96	0	.01	.04	.01	0	0	0	0
foot	97.23	0	.01	0	0	2.07	0	.16	.02	.43	.05	0	.02	0
19. Tablespoon (74.120a)														
bowl (reverse)	88.28	.02	.03	.04	.04	11.04	0	.26	.10	.12	.02	0	0	.06
handle (obverse)	89.53	.01	.03	.04	.04	9.86	0	.24	.08	.13	.02	0	.02	0
Tablespoon (74.120b)														
bowl (reverse)	88.54	0	.02	.02	.04	10.84	0	.26	.09	.14	.01	0	0	0
handle (obverse)	89.22	.02	.03	.01	.03	10.20	0	.25	.08	.14	.01	0	.01	0

Entry	Ag	Mn	Fe	Co	Ni	Cu	As	Pb	Zn	Au	Hg	Cd	Sn	Sb
20. Cross (52.212)														
crossing (reverse)	93.01	0	.02	.02	.02	6.56	0	.19	.05	.10	.01	0	.01	0
upper arm (obverse)	94.45	.01	.02	.02	.01	5.17	0	.18	.03	.09	.01	0	0	0
lower arm (obverse)	94.61	.01	.02	.02	.01	4.94	0	.22	.03	.11	.01	0	.02	0
21. Cross of Lorraine (52.223)														
lower arm	96.10	0	.03	.05	.01	3.44	0	.16	.02	.10	.02	0	.04	0
Beaver ornament (73.198) [By Robert Cruickshank]														
top	95.23	0	.03	0	.01	4.17	.01	.27	.05	.19	.02	0	.01	0
24. Reliquary cross (57.141)														
crossing (obverse)	87.03	.01	.08	.06	.04	12.17	0	.29	.19	.08	.02	0	.03	0
crossing (reverse)	89.08	.02	.04	.04	.03	10.19	0	.28	.22	.06	.01	0	.03	0
25. Ciborium (69.263)														
cover	92.34	0	.03	.01	.02	6.84	.01	.25	.09	.35	.04	0	.01	0
bowl (outside)	93.62	0	.01	.03	.02	5.53	.01	.23	.08	.40	.06	0	0	0
bowl (inside, gilt)	63.90	.04	.12	.16	.12	2.61	.20	.50	.44	24.76	7.06	0	.09	0
knop	94.02	0	.03	0	.02	4.99	.02	.34	.07	.43	.05	0	.02	0
foot	92.72	0	.02	0	.02	6.46	.01	.24	.08	.38	.04	0	.02	0
26. Holy water stoup (69.261)														
bucket	92.03	0	.04	.03	.03	7.37	.03	.21	.08	.15	.02	0	.01	0
handle	95.48	0	.01	0	0	3.99	.01	.21	.06	.18	.02	0	.03	0
Sprinkler (69.262)														
handle	91.66	0	.02	.02	.02	7.64	0	.30	.14	.14	.02	0	.02	0

Entry	Ag	Mn	Fe	Co	Ni	Cu	As	Pb	Zn	Au	Hg	Cd	Sn	Sb
27. Incense-boat (74.4)														
lid (front)	96.18	0	.02	0	.01	3.35	0	.35	.01	.04	.01	0	.02	0
boat	95.66	0	.02	0	.02	3.78	.02	.42	.02	.04	.01	.01	.01	0
basal rim	93.82	0	.03	.02	.02	5.70	0	.25	.09	.02	.01	.01	.02	0
28. Tablespoon (69.173)														
bowl (reverse)	91.91	.02	.03	.03	.03	7.20	0	.38	.11	.25	.03	0	.01	0
handle (obverse)	92.90	.01	.02	.04	.02	6.28	0	.37	.09	.23	.02	0	.02	0
Tablespoon (69.174)														
bowl (reverse)	92.58	.02	.02	.02	.04	6.63	0	.34	.10	.24	.02	0	0	0
handle (obverse)	93.46	.01	.03	.01	.02	5.83	0	.31	.08	.20	.02	0	.02	0
30. Tumbler (49.406)														
side	95.12	.01	.01	.03	.01	4.35	0	.26	.04	.11	.02	0	.02	.01
rim (repair)	94.03	0	.02	.03	.02	5.44	0	.31	.05	.08	.01	0	.01	0
31. Ciborium (69.264)														
cover	99.03	0	.16	.02	0	.40	0	.20	.01	.11	.04	0	.03	0
bowl (outside)	94.66	0	.02	0	.02	4.36	0	.39	.04	.47	.05	0	0	0
bowl (inside, gilt)	57.44	.07	.13	.21	.16	3.18	.52	1.15	.56	30.34	6.12	0	.04	.07
knop	99.75	0	0	0	0	.14	0	.05	.01	.04	.01	0	0	0
foot (top)	99.06	0	0	.02	0	.38	0	.32	.02	.10	.02	0	.08	0
foot (underneath)	98.21	0	0	.01	.01	.94	0	.52	.02	.15	.03	0	.08	0
foot (underneath, after polishing)	97.94	0	0	0	0	1.22	0	.55	.02	.16	.03	0	.08	0
foot (underneath, after sanding)	97.39	0	.02	0	.02	1.88	0	.40	.05	.13	.03	0	.09	0
Plate (72.223) [Attributed to Jean-François Landron]														
obverse (rim)	95.94	.01	.03	.02	.01	3.79	0	.14	.03	0	0	0	.02	0
reverse	96.13	0	.01	.01	0	3.71	0	.10	.02	0	0	0	0	0

Entry	Ag	Mn	Fe	Co	Ni	Cu	As	Pb	Zn	Au	Hg	Cd	Sn	Sb
32. Chalice (57.143)														
cup (outside)	93.58	0	0	.03	.02	5.76	0	.28	.12	.14	.04	0	.01	0
knop	95.03	0	.02	.02	.01	4.42	0	.22	.04	.19	.02	0	.02	0
foot	93.68	.02	.02	.03	.02	5.77	0	.22	.06	.11	.02	0	.03	0
33. Ciborium (57.144)														
cover	90.09	0	.04	.04	.02	8.73	.01	.19	.16	.58	.08	0	.05	0
bowl (outside)	93.83	0	.01	0	.01	4.80	.02	.18	.10	.92	.11	0	0	0
bowl (inside, gilt)	87.77	.02	.03	.04	.05	7.00	.04	.30	.22	3.86	.65	0	.01	.01
knop	92.22	0	.03	0	.02	6.53	.02	.25	.19	.67	.07	0	0	0
foot	92.91	0	.03	.02	.03	6.43	.01	.15	.07	.28	.03	0	.03	0
34. Snuff box (74.119)														
top	92.67	0	.02	.02	.02	7.04	0	.15	.04	0	0	0	.02	0
bottom	92.99	0	.01	.02	.03	6.71	0	.17	.04	0	.01	0	.02	0
35. Écuelle (46.350)														
bottom	94.45	.01	.01	.03	.02	4.93	0	.14	.04	.33	.02	0	.01	0
handle (reverse)	93.66	.01	.02	.02	.03	5.78	0	.25	.04	.17	.01	0	.01	0
36. Écuelle (61.7)														
bottom	92.32	.01	.03	.02	.04	7.14	0	.16	.08	.16	.01	0	.03	0
handle (obverse)	92.95	.01	.02	.02	.03	6.51	0	.20	.08	.13	.02	0	.02	0
37. Tablespoon (52.240)														
bowl (reverse)	75.06	.02	.06	.08	.08	24.11	.02	.21	.21	.09	.02	0	.03	0
handle (obverse)	78.77	.02	.08	.08	.08	20.43	.01	.22	.16	.08	.02	0	.03	.01

Entry	Ag	Mn	Fe	Co	Ni	Cu	As	Pb	Zn	Au	Hg	Cd	Sn	Sb
38. Holy water stoup														
(69.300a)														
bucket	91.97	0	.03	.04	.04	7.30	0	.04	.10	.38	0	0	.09	0
foot (front)	92.26	0	.02	.02	.03	7.24	0	.05	.10	.26	.01	0	0	0
foot (back)	92.58	0	.03	.07	.04	6.76	0	.04	.08	.31	.01	0	.08	0
handle	97.40	0	.02	.05	.02	2.23	0	.02	.03	.03	0	.04	.15	0
Sprinkler (69.300b)														
head	91.89	.01	.01	.03	.02	7.85	0	.04	.11	.03	0	0	0	0
handle	93.25	.01	.02	.02	.02	6.59	0	.03	.04	0	0	0	.02	0
39. Tablespoon (50.131)														
bowl (reverse)	90.08	.01	.03	.02	.04	9.39	0	.22	.08	.10	.01	0	0	.02
handle (obverse)	90.96	.01	.06	.02	.03	8.50	0	.21	.06	.11	.01	0	.02	0
Tablespoon (50.132)														
bowl (reverse)	90.68	0	.04	.03	.02	8.91	0	.14	.06	.09	.01	0	0	0
handle (obverse)	91.61	.02	.04	.03	.03	7.95	0	.14	.05	.09	.01	0	.02	0
40. Gorget (64.87)														
center (obverse)	88.62	.01	.02	.04	.04	10.84	.03	.20	.07	.09	.02	0	0	0
41. Tablespoon (61.188)														
bowl (reverse)	92.27	.01	.02	0	.01	7.28	0	.23	.04	.11	.01	0	0	0
handle (obverse)	92.73	.01	.03	.02	.02	6.79	0	.23	.04	.12	.01	0	.01	0
43. Ciborium (74.3)														
cover	96.42	0	.02	0	0	3.17	0	.15	.02	.16	.04	0	.01	0
bowl (outside)	96.16	0	.01	0	.01	3.39	0	.15	.02	.21	.04	0	0	0
bowl (inside, gilt)	91.04	.01	.03	.04	.03	5.49	.03	.15	.08	2.74	.30	.01	.06	0
knop	94.01	0	.03	0	.02	5.42	.02	.18	.03	.25	.03	0	0	0
foot	95.98	0	.02	0	0	3.54	0	.16	.05	.18	.05	0	.01	0

Entry	Ag	Mn	Fe	Co	Ni	Cu	As	Pb	Zn	Au	Hg	Cd	Sn	Sb
44. Ciborium (70.719)														
cover (gilt)	87.81	0	.04	0	.04	7.26	.04	.21	.14	4.03	.39	0	.03	0
bowl (outside, gilt)	91.09	0	.03	0	.03	6.54	.02	.19	.08	1.84	.17	0	.01	0
bowl (inside, gilt)	91.70	0	.03	.02	.02	6.78	.01	.19	.06	1.03	.11	.01	.04	0
knop (gilt)	91.65	0	.03	.02	.03	6.05	.03	.21	.07	1.74	.17	0	0	0
foot (gilt)	91.58	0	.03	.02	.02	5.15	.03	.19	.08	2.63	.25	0	.01	0
45. Fork (69.526)														
tines (reverse, base)	91.83	0	.03	.02	.02	7.78	0	.19	.05	.05	.01	0	.02	0
handle (reverse)	91.29	.02	.16	.04	.02	8.13	0	.21	.05	.06	.01	0	0	0
47. Ladle (49.22)														
bowl (reverse)	90.72	.01	.02	.03	.03	8.34	0	.47	.16	.18	.02	0	.01	0
handle (obverse)	90.30	.01	.03	.04	.03	8.80	0	.45	.16	.15	.02	0	0	0

Glossary

Ajouré	*See* Openwork.
Ampulla	A small, often cylindrical container for holy oil (chrism).
Annealing	Heating the silver to keep it malleable when being worked.
Anthemion	A stylized motif derived from the honeysuckle; of classical Greek origin.
Applied	Attached by brazing; small separately fashioned elements were often applied to vessels.
Baluster stem	A stem with an outline derived from the architectural turned baluster or post of a balustrade.
Bead	A small, continuous, half-round convex molding.
Bead and reel	Decorative edging consisting of alternating beads and reels.
Beading	A series of small half-spheres.
Bezel	The inside rim of the bowl or lid of a vessel which secures the lid.
Boss	A roundish or convex ornament raised from the surface of the metal.
Brazed	Soldered or joined by means of a brazing solder; brazing solder is hard solder with a high melting point (soft solders have a low melting point) and consists of an alloy of silver, copper, and zinc.
Bright-cut	Engraved by means of short shallow strokes at an angle to create a faceted effect.
Burnished	Polished with a burnisher, a tool with a hard, polished working surface, such as agate or dog's tooth.
Cable molding	A molding resembling twisted rope.
Calyx	An ornamental cup-like section which partially or completely encloses the cup of a chalice or bowl of a ciborium; also known as a collar.

167

Cartouche	A decorative framing device enclosing initials, an inscription, or a coat of arms.	Engrailed	Edged with a series of concave notches.
Cavetto	A concave quarter-circle molding.	Engraving	Ornament or initials formed by cutting fine lines into silver with a scorper or graver.
Chasing	Modeling the surface by hammering and punching, without removing any metal, to achieve linear patterns or matte effects.	False knop	A flange, small bulb, or boss below (and sometimes above) the knop of a baluster stem; derived from the French *faux-noeud. See also* Collar knop; Cushion knop.
Cipher	Initials, interwoven and repeated in reverse, forming a balanced design.		
Collar knop	A small flange-like knop, usually with decorative edging, found above and (or) below the large knop of a baluster stem.	Feather edge	A type of bright-cut ornament consisting of a narrow band of wedge-shaped facets used as ornamental edging and simulating gadrooning.
Console	A curved ornamental bracket with scrolled end(s).	Festoon	A pendant garland of flowers, fruit, etc.; also any looped ornament in a series.
Cushion knop	A small bulb-like knop with flattened top and bottom, found above and (or) below the large knop of a baluster stem.	Fillet	A flat, narrow band.
		Finial	The uppermost, often knob-like, terminal of an object.
Cyma reversa	An S-curve molding, the upper curve convex, the lower concave; also known as a reverse ogee molding.	Flange	A thin, horizontal, projecting rim or edge.
Diaperwork	Pattern of repeated diamonds or lozenges.	Fluting	A series of long, parallel, concave channels; the opposite of reeding.
Dentiled	Edged with a series of small tooth-like projections.	Gadrooning	A series of long, convex, parallel lobes or bosses.
Drawn	Shaped by pulling a strip of silver through an aperture in a drawplate; narrow moldings and bands are fashioned in this manner.	Gilding	A thin layer of gold applied by one of two methods: in mercury (amalgam) gilding an amalgam of mercury and gold is coated on the surface and then heated, causing the mercury to evaporate and the gold to fuse to the silver; in electro-gilding (electrolysis) the object is immersed in a solution containing gold ions.
Écuelle	A shallow two-handled soup bowl or porringer, often made with a cover and plate in France but usually alone in Canada.		
Egg and dart	Ornament of alternating ovolos and arrowheads.	Knop	The large knob or bulb of a baluster stem.
Electro-gilt	*See* Gilding.	Lavabo	The basin used in the ritual washing of the priest's hands during the Mass.
Embossing	Relief ornament formed by raising the surface of the metal from the reverse side, as with a hammer.	Maker's mark	A silversmith's identifying mark; in the early eighteenth century it usually

	consisted of the silversmith's initials and a device or devices such as a fleur-de-lis, crown, crescent, star, pellets, etc.; by the late eighteenth century usually it was initials only; in the early nineteenth century the surname was sometimes used with or without the first initial.
Matting	A dull textured surface created by chasing or punching minute indentations close together.
Openwork	Ornament formed by piercing or cutting openings in the metal.
Parcel gilt	Partially gilt.
Pax	A small devotional plaque with a religious image on the front; this was kissed by the clergy and congregation during the Mass.
Piscina	*See* Lavabo.
Planishing	Smoothing the surface of the metal with a flat-faced hammer to remove the irregularities caused by the original shaping.
Pyx	A small traveling case for Eucharistic wafers, sometimes in the form of a miniature ciborium.
Raising	Shaping a thin disc of silver into a hollow form by hammering it on an anvil-like raising stake.
Reeding	A series of thin parallel convex ribs; the opposite of fluting.
Repoussé	*See* Embossing.
Rouletting	An engraved zigzag pattern, often found on Indian trade silver.
Scalloped	Edged in a series of curves or circle segments.
Seamed	Joined by brazing together two (or more) edges.
Silverplating	Originally, the fusing of thin sheets of silver with a thick sheet of copper, as in Sheffield plate; after about 1840, the electrodepositing of a thin layer of silver on a base metal, more often a nickel-silver alloy.
Sinking	The technique of shaping a thin disc of silver by hammering it into the hollow of a block of wood.
Soleil	The sunburst or glory of a monstrance.
Spun	Shaped by pressing a tool against a revolving silver sheet mounted on the chuck of a lathe.
Strapwork	Ornament consisting of straps or ribbons, either applied, chased, or engraved.
Swaged	Shaped by hammering the metal into a swage or negative die.
Torus	A large half-round convex molding.

Index

Ross Allan C. Fox was a curatorial associate at The Detroit Institute of Arts when this catalogue was being prepared. He is now continuing his research at the University of Missouri.

The manuscript was prepared for publication by Jean Owen. The book was designed by Don Ross. The typeface for the text is Mergenthaler's Times Roman, designed under the supervision of Stanley Morison in 1931. The display face is Caslon, based on an original design by William Caslon of about 1725.

The text is printed on 70 lb. S. D. Warren's Patina paper, and the book is bound in Holliston Kingston cloth over binder's boards. Manufactured in the United States of America.